Hope this hel
Day! ♡you

To:

_____

From:

_____

Date:

_____

DayBook
of
Faith

God's Presence in Your Day

Jan L. Dargatz

PUBLISHING GROUP
Nashville, Tennessee

DayBook of Faith

God's Presence in Your Day

Copyright © 2014 Jan L. Dargatz

ISBN: 978-1-4336-8161-5

Published by B&H Publishing Group, Nashville, Tennessee

Dewey Decimal Classification: 242.64

Subject Heading: DEVOTIONAL LITERATURE \ FAITH \ CHRISTIAN LIFE

Packager Development: Meadow's Edge Group LLC

Scripture quotations are taken from the Holman Christian Standard Bible® (HCSB®), Copyright © 1999, 2000, 2002, 2003 by Holman Bible Publishers. Used by permission. Holman Christian Standard Bible®, Holman CSB®, and HCSB® are federally registered trademarks of Holman Bible Publishers.

Printed in China

1 2 3 4 5 6 7 8 • 18 17 16 15 14

Packager Development: Meadow's Edge Group LLC
Designed by ThinkpenDesign.com

TABLE OF CONTENTS

Introduction 7

Through Life's Twists and Turns 12

Everything in Vivid Detail 14

What Percentage? 16

Arms of Loving Embrace 18

A Supply of Wisdom. 20

Even Better Than Requested . . . 22

Exactly the Direction Needed . . 24

Who Makes It Happen? 26

Let the Oven Do Its Work. . . . 28

The Slow Track 30

Faith to Let Go 32

The Shortest Lecture. 34

From Where I Am 36

Necessities 38

Rise and Make Up Your Bed . . . 40

As They Were Going. 42

Faith Goals 44

Finding the Fulcrum 46

One Foggy Night. 48

A Bit at a Time 50

A Different Team? 52

Upstream Paddling 54

No Shifting 56

The West Bank at Midnight. . . . 58

Nothing . . . or Everything 60

He Hasn't Moved. 62

Sleeping Like a Baby. 64

The Lumberjack 66

Factored In 68

Going with God 70

Persevering in God's Answers . . 72

Miracles, Not Magic. 74

Thirty-Four Years 76

Faith for Right Now 78

God's Property 80

Stay Connected. 82

A Bazillionth Chance 84

A Divine Turnaround 86

Backstage Success 88

A Family Commitment 90

Family Faith Goals. 92

Faith to Stand Firm 94

Go for the Perfect Fit 96

God Believes in You 98

Mutual Expectations 100

Visibility 102

Being Faith-FULL 104

Driving on the Road of Faith . . 106

Profile of the Faithful 108

Which Way? 110

Change! 112

"Get Off My Porch!" 114

Rescue Assured 116

Words of Faith 118

Faith for the Small Things . . . 120

Thanks and Trust 122

Home Run Faith 124

Heaven Bound 126

Preparing for the Test 128

Extreme Skateboarder. 130

The Focus of Faith 132

A Way through the Maze 134

Prayer for Faith. 136

A Better Blessing. 138

No Substitute for Deciding . . . 140

Day-by-Day Faith 142

Faithalistic 144

In Alignment. 146

God's Invitation 148

A Spiritual Knowing. 150

Faith for Dying. 152

A Working Definition 154

A Faith Pact. 156

"I'll Do the Believing". 158

What God Requires 160

The Reluctant Preacher 162

A New Understanding. 164

Put to the Test 166

Fifteen Questions 168

Mustard Seed. 170

What God Can Do. 172

Claiming What Is Important. . .174

A New Start. 176

David-Style Faith. 178

Walking the Walk 180

The Moments Add Up. 182

A Vision for What Might Be . . 184

Pouring Faith into a New Goal. 186

Renewed Eyes of Faith. 188

Seeing as God Sees. 190

Bottom-Line Faith 192

A Faith Story 194

A Prime Faith Moment 196

Your Heroes of Faith. 198

The Concert Surprise 200

God's Divine Tugging 202

Faith-Inspiring Scripture to

    Memorize. 204

INTRODUCTION

A MEASURE OF FAITH

God has distributed a measure of faith to each one.

(ROMANS 12:3)

*T*he Bible tells us that God has given to *every* person a measure of faith—a *degree* of "ability to believe."

Some people seem to believe quite easily, even to the point where others might regard them as gullible or susceptible to easy manipulation. Those who "believe quickly" often believe what others say at face value, try anything they are encouraged to try—believing they can succeed at it—and fail to ask discerning questions to confirm the wisdom of what they are being told. While they are sometimes disappointed or deceived, in many cases those who "believe quickly" see tremendous miracles in their lives and are quick to thank and praise God.

In contrast, those who have difficulty believing are often perceived as inflexible, suspicious, hard-hearted, or too cautious. Those who "believe slowly" sometimes have become that way because others have tricked them or misled them in the past. While they often make wise choices in their caution, they sometimes miss engaging in spontaneous acts of kindness that might bring great joy to them and to others.

Is there a middle ground? Most assuredly. God desires for our faith to have a solid foundation based *solely* on His goodness, love, promises, and presence. God's nature does not change; His mercy is extended to all. God also desires for us to use our faith—it is the key to giving God full entrée into our lives to do His work in us, through us, and for us!

The Bible also challenges us to GROW in faith. And the good news about our ability to grow is this: we each have the *capacity to grow*. Our starting point in faith is never intended to be our ending point!

The worthy goal, therefore, is to believe those things that God wants us to believe:

Examine Your Beliefs: The Scriptures teach us that we are wise to test all information—to confirm what we hear against what God has commanded or promised.

We are to ask questions with an honest and eager willingness to find answers and apply them. And, we are *not* to allow others to dissuade us from doing good, no matter how many times a person or group of people disappoints us or attempts to discourage us.

The word most commonly used for faith in the New Testament is *pistis* (PIS-tis). It comes from the Greek word *peitho*, which means "to persuade." True Christian faith means being completely persuaded that there is no other truth apart from the Word of God. Only a belief based on the Word creates a foundation for ongoing faithfulness.

Grow in Your Understanding: We are encouraged in Scripture to pursue those things God authorizes or compels us to pursue. We are to *desire* to grow in faith.

The best "food" for our faith is always going to be the Word of God—not only the written Word of God (the Bible) but also the life examples of Jesus (the "Word" in John 1:1), and the word of God spoken to us as we pray, contemplate God's purposes, and listen for the Spirit of God to give us wise counsel.

Avail yourself of the opportunity to grow in your faith by reading God's Word daily, by praying daily and spending time listening for the Lord to speak to you, and by asking yourself repeatedly on any given day, "How would Jesus approach this problem, this relationship, this experience, or this opportunity?"

At all times, ask the Lord to "teach you" how to better follow Him.

Apply Your Faith to Real Life: The person who has faith rooted firmly in the Word of God is a person who is in a prime position to APPLY faith to every circumstance of life—every situation, every relationship, every difficulty, *every time*!

We are to say in the face of every need and opportunity: "What would God desire for me to say or do as an act of my TRUST in Him?"

Faith that Generates Trust: Faith is often associated with specific acts or statements that reflect belief. A faith-filled word of encouragement . . . a hand outstretched in comfort . . . a prayer . . . a helpful deed . . . these are set in time and space like diamonds that reflect God's glory.

TRUST is a *pattern of faith*. Trust is faith that is ongoing, and that is consistent.

Trust and love go hand-in-hand to create a deepening relationship with God. Trust accepts completely that God is sovereign over His universe—that He is omnipotent (all-powerful), omniscient (all-knowing and all-wise), omnipresent (in the moment and eternal), and all-loving (to all people). Trust looks to God for mercy, forgiveness, and all things necessary for godly living.

The person who trusts God and who engages in acts of faith will soon find that God is faithful to His Word and His promises. He protects . . . He provides . . . He comforts . . . He heals and delivers . . . He restores and reconciles . . . He makes us *whole*.

The more we trust, the more God shows Himself trustworthy. And in that cycle of trust and trustwortiness, we *grow*—not only in faith but in the character likeness of Christ Jesus.

We not only become a person of faith, we become a *faithful person*!

Faith and Faithfulnes Are Linked: The more we embrace God's faithfulness, the more we desire to be faithful to Him in return. And the quicker we are to apply our faith and trust God with *all* the consequences.

The stories of others can be a tremendous source of inspiration to us when it comes to understanding and applying our faith. That is the purpose of this book. It draws from nature, history, the Bible, and mostly from the everyday life examples of other people to send a message: "Trust God! He *will* help you. He *will* use you. He *will* reward you for your belief in Him."

A Renewable Resource: Read the devotionals in this book with a *belief* that your faith is a renewable, rechargeable resource. Make a choice to read these pages repeatedly, and at each reading, look for a new way to apply the kernels of truth and inspiration to *your* life.

Faith *always* functions simultaneously at the "today" and the "eternal" levels of human existence. What you draw from eternity as truth for your day will build your faith *now*. What you do *now* as an act of faith will impact your future in eternity.

Today is always a day for faith in action!

—*Jan Dargatz, PhD*

Through Life's Twists and Turns

The earth and everything in it, the world and
its inhabitants, belong to the Lord;
for He laid its foundation on the seas
and established it on the rivers.

(Psalm 24:1–2)

The Jordan River in Israel is mentioned in the Bible nearly two hundred times!

The Jordan flows through a land area that extends sixty-five miles from the south shore of the Sea of Galilee to the Dead Sea. The river itself, however, winds back and forth so that it is almost two hundred miles long. The river drops significantly in altitude from sea to sea—more than six hundred feet, with a number of "rapids" segments in otherwise calm river waters.

The Bible tells that the river's waters parted in Joshua's day to allow the children of Israel to cross on dry ground. Naaman was cured of leprosy after dipping in the river seven times. Elijah was taken into heaven after crossing the Jordan River. In Elisha's time, a heavy ax head floated to the river's surface. Jesus was baptized in the Jordan River.

The Jordan River's main purpose through the centuries, however, has not been to provide a setting for dramatic miracles. The river's *purpose* has been to provide life-giving water to the people, livestock, and crops grown along its banks. The waters of the river have made the Jordan River Valley one of the most fertile and fruitful valleys in the world.

In many ways, the Jordan is a metaphor for our faith.

No person ever has a totally "straight shot" of success through life. Every person has twists and turns that can threaten to move a person off course from their God-given purpose. Every person has ups and downs that challenge their faith. Even so, every person's life is marked by miracles that must be recognized as coming from God's hand. Our purpose throughout life is to provide a life-giving message to the world—to produce spiritual fruit and to give witness to the eternal life offered by God.

BE A SOURCE OF LIFE-GIVING REFRESHMENT TODAY!

EVERYTHING IN VIVID DETAIL

The fear of the LORD
is the beginning of wisdom,
and the knowledge of the
Holy One is understanding.

(PROVERBS 9:10)

One of the words that has been used to describe God for thousands of years is "omniscient." The word means "all-wise" or "all-knowing."

God, who created everything, knows even the most minute details about every aspect of His creation. He *knows* that you blink your eyes an average of twelve times a minute . . . that the hardest substance in your body is tooth enamel . . . and that the iris of your eyes is unlike that of any other person on the planet.

God knows that no two sunsets or snowflakes are identical. He knows that all muscles function in pairs and that it was important to give camels two sets of eyelashes.

God knows that He has made 350 *trillion* galaxies, and He knows the number of stars and planets in each one of them. He knows when the weather is going to begin to change from one season to the next. He knows *how* to make a seed germinate, and how long it will take to produce a harvest.

God knows the precise air currents to help an eagle soar, how to coordinate the 228 muscles in the head of a caterpillar, and how to help a spider spin sixty feet of silk in an hour.

God knows the number of hairs on your head. He knows what you dreamed last night and what you are going through right now. He knows all of the things that He has planned for your life, and how to make them happen. He knows how to produce in you the character likeness of Christ Jesus.

You don't need to know everything! You only need to know you are in relationship with the One who does know everything!

TRUST GOD TO REVEAL TO YOU THE DETAILS YOU NEED TO KNOW, WHEN YOU NEED TO KNOW THEM.

What Percentage?

[Jesus said,] "Love the Lord your God with all your heart, with all your soul, with all your mind, and with all your strength."

(Mark 12:30)

The Bible tells about a day when Jesus was in the outer courtyard of the temple in Jerusalem, "watching" as people dropped their financial offerings into one of the large inverted trumpet-shaped containers located there. He saw the rich throw in large sums, usually in ways that led others to take note of the clatter caused by their many coins. He also saw a woman, a "poor widow," contribute two small copper coins—an amount that would not even be equal to a penny in American money today.

Jesus commented, "This poor widow has put in more than all those giving to the temple treasury. For they all gave out of their surplus, but she out of her poverty has put in everything she possessed—all she had to live on" (Mark 12:43–44).

This woman gave *everything*. The rich contributors apparently gave only a small percentage of the "excess" they had—rarely did people give more than the 10 percent (tithe) required by the law of Moses. This woman gave *100 percent*!

Some say it was foolish for her to give everything. "How could she support herself?" they ask. The reality is, two small copper coins wouldn't have been enough for her to purchase *anything* other than a small round of pita bread. It certainly wasn't enough money for a day's worth of food, any form of lodging, or any other goods or services she might have needed.

In giving everything to the Lord, she was surrendering *her entire being.* She made herself totally dependent upon God. She trusted Him to care for her in the same way He provided for the sparrows and the field flowers—solely because she was His beloved creation.

What percentage of your life are you entrusting to God today? Is it everything, or just a part?

GOD WANTS ALL OF US, ALL THE TIME.

ARMS OF LOVING EMBRACE

Do not fear, for I am with you;
do not be afraid, for I am your God.
I will strengthen you; I will help you;
I will hold on to you with My righteous right hand.

(ISAIAH 41:10)

Seven-year-old Robby's world was turned upside down when his father died in a car accident and, shortly thereafter, his mother became seriously ill. Although the friends and relatives taking care of Robby understood the reasons for his sudden outbursts of anger and frantic behavior, none of them knew how to deal with his "acting out" episodes. They consulted a special counselor at Robby's school.

The counselor spent some time observing Robby. When Robby went into one of his "out of control" episodes, she calmly went to him and quietly but firmly took hold of his arms and looked him directly in the eyes with great love and compassion. He looked back in fear, expecting to be punished. Instead, the counselor said, "Robby, when children act this way I hold them like this until they get quiet inside."

Robby stopped struggling and after a few moments said, "You can let go now. I won't do that again."

The counselor said, "Okay," and let him go.

The next day, however, Robby went into another angry tirade, this time with one eye on the counselor. She walked slowly toward him as she had the day before, but before she could reach Robby, he suddenly grabbed his own arms in a self-embrace and said, "You don't have to hold me. I can hold myself." And he did.

We all need to learn to discipline ourselves at times and "hold ourselves" from frantic responses to a world that may seem to be spinning out of control around us. As we embrace *ourselves*, we can know by faith that we are being held even more tightly in the everlasting arms of a loving Father, who will never leave us, abandon us, or punish us for our fears.

LET GOD'S EMBRACE COMFORT AND SHIELD YOU!

A Supply of Wisdom

Now if any of you lacks wisdom, he should ask God, who
gives to all generously and without criticizing, and it will be
given to him. But let him ask in faith without doubting.

(James 1:5–6)

A missionary to Mongolia, James Gilmour, was surprised the day several wounded soldiers were brought to him for care. Gilmour was not a doctor, but he did have some knowledge of first aid, so he agreed to help the men the best he could. He cleaned and dressed the wounds of two of the soldiers but discovered that the third man's leg was badly broken. He had no idea how to help him.

He knelt beside the man, humbly asking God for guidance. Then he rose, confident that somehow God would send help for the situation. Within a matter of minutes, a group of beggars walking on the road beside the mission station approached Gilmour to ask him for money. His heart went out to them and he hurriedly gave them each a small gift of money and a few encouraging words.

One beggar remained behind as the others left. Gilmour noted that the man was so thin he seemed to be nothing but skin draped over bones. He concluded that the man simply didn't have the energy or strength to walk any farther. He thought, *This man is a walking skeleton.* And in thinking that thought, he suddenly realized God had sent him a living anatomy lesson! He asked the beggar if he could examine him and the man agreed.

Gilmour carefully traced the man's femur bone with his fingers, and discovered what he needed to do to set the soldier's broken leg.

When we come to God with a humble heart, admitting we don't know what to do but trusting Him to provide answers from His unlimited supply of wisdom, God *will* answer us and show us the way. The Lord has promised never to reject an honest request for vital information, if we ask in faith.

GOD HAS THE ANSWERS YOU NEED FOR TODAY!

EVEN BETTER THAN REQUESTED

*Now this is the confidence we have before Him: Whenever
we ask anything according to His will, He hears us.
And if we know that He hears whatever we ask, we
know that we have what we have asked Him for.*

(1 JOHN 5:14–15)

*A*unt Joan couldn't help but notice that her young niece Ella
was upset about something. Her niece was normally an even-
tempered, calm child, but on this particular day she couldn't seem to
focus her attention, even as she played. Every few minutes, Ella seemed
to embark on a search for something—looking under sofa cushions,
behind furniture, and inside cabinets and drawers. Aunt Joan finally
asked, "Is something wrong, Ella? Did you lose something?"

Ella replied with big tears in her eyes, "Oh, yes! I lost Babby's shoes.
I've looked everywhere, Aunt Joan. Babby *has* to have her shoes!"

Knowing that Babby was Ella's favorite baby doll, and recognizing
that this loss was important to her young niece, Aunt Joan called her
to come sit beside her in the big overstuffed chair where they often sat
to read, talk, or pray together.

As she hugged Ella, with Babby in Ella's lap, Aunt Joan said, "Why
don't we pray about this, Ella? God knows *exactly* where Babby's shoes
are hiding. Let's ask God to show us where they are."

Together, they prayed, and Ella grew calm. She resumed her busy afternoon of play, complete with happy imaginary conversations with Babby.

The next day, Aunt Joan was almost afraid to bring up the missing doll shoes, but she finally asked, "Ella, did you find Babby's shoes?"

"No," Ella said with unexpected good cheer. "But God made me not want to find them. It's summer, and I decided Babby would rather go barefoot!"

We don't always receive from God what we *thought* we wanted when we made our initial prayer request. Sometimes God changes our desires, and sometimes He gives us something *even better* than what we requested. His plan—creative, timely, and purpose filled—is always for our good.

Expect God's best ideas!

EXACTLY THE DIRECTION NEEDED

I am Yahweh your God,
who teaches you for your benefit,
who leads you in the way you should go.

(ISAIAH 48:17)

*J*oe readily admitted that he was directionally challenged. He wouldn't dream of going any place without his GPS device. His friends teased him that he liked the soft feminine voice of his GPS "advisor," but in truth, Joe found the woman's voice irritating at times. He especially hated to hear her words, "You have missed your turn. Recalculating!"

Normally, Joe's electronic passenger was especially valuable to him on long road trips. But on one occasion, she began informing him that he needed to stop and get gasoline—long before Joe thought such a stop was necessary. "Your fuel level is low," the voice cooed. Joe just smiled and drove on, confident that he had another fifty miles of gasoline available.

Every few minutes, however, Miss GPS spoke again, and finally, Joe had heard enough. He unplugged "her" and sat back to relax in peace, grateful to be free of what he perceived to be rather incessant nagging.

A few miles later, his car began sputtering, and just as Joe pulled to the edge of the highway, the car died. Sure enough, he was out of gas! It didn't help that the roadside service vehicle that came to his assistance a half hour later was driven by a woman—who had a voice amazingly similar to that of Miss GPS!

God knows what we need *in advance* of our knowing. He has already provided all that we each need to walk in His ways and bring glory to His name *today*. Our part is to listen with faith to His still small voice telling us what to say and do, where and when to go, and how to receive all that He desires to give.

GOD IS OUR NEVER-FAIL VOICE
OF GLOBAL POSITIONING!

WHO MAKES IT HAPPEN?

*[Jesus said,] "I am the Alpha and the Omega, the First
and the Last, the Beginning and the End."*
(REVELATION 22:13)

One windy Sunday morning, a children's pastor gathered the children of the church around him at the front of the church and told about a boy who had been given a prize in a citywide kite-flying contest. He was given the prize for having the most beautiful kite that had soared for the longest time period above the city's central park.

The mayor, in presenting the award, asked, "Who is responsible for the amazing flight of this beautiful kite?"

The little boy quickly said, "I am! I made this kite with my own hands from scraps I found in my dad's workshop. I painted the pictures on it myself. I ran down the field until the kite took off, and I guided it with the string."

The mayor smiled and nodded, but then the wind spoke up, "No! I am responsible! I was the force that kept this kite in the sky. If I had not blown, this kite could not have flown at all!"

The mayor then heard a third voice. The kite's tail spoke up, "I am responsible. I made the kite sail on the currents of the wind and gave stability to the kite. Without me, the boy could not have saved the kite from crashing to the ground."

The pastor asked the children, "Now, who do *you* say flew the kite?"

Several of the children spoke up simultaneously, "All three!"

Things happen in our lives in part because of what *we* do, and most certainly because of what *God provides and allows.* They also happen with the help or permission of others around us. Be thankful for those God has sent to assist you, for God's enabling power and creativity, and for God who sets up the perfect circumstances for your success.

HAVE FAITH THAT GOD IS ULTIMATELY IN
CHARGE OF ALL THE PEOPLE, PROJECTS,
AND CIRCUMSTANCES IN YOUR LIFE!

LET THE OVEN DO ITS WORK

All who wait patiently for Him are happy.

(ISAIAH 30:18)

*L*indy loved to bake with Grandma. She liked every part of the process—choosing a recipe and setting out and putting together all the ingredients. She especially liked the *eating* of the baked goods she and Grandma made!

Of all the things they baked together, Lindy most enjoyed making three-layer chocolate cakes. The cakes took several hours to make, including letting the cake cool after baking so the layers might be iced, combined, and then covered in Grandma's extra-special chocolate cream frosting.

One thing that Lindy did *not* enjoy was waiting for the cake layers to bake. She got into a bad habit. "I just want to make sure they're cooking," she'd say as she popped open the oven door before Grandma could protest.

Finally Grandma said, "Lindy, I would be a very poor cake-baking teacher if I didn't tell you something." Linday was eager to listen. Grandma said, "When you open the oven door you let in a blast of cold air. That can cause the cake to fall if it is rising, which will make for a tough texture and *slow* the baking time. A cake needs to bake in an even temperature without any interference." And then

Grandma added a phrase Lindy never forgot: *"You need to let the oven do its work."*

A few Sundays after this talk, Linda was at church with Grandma. The pastor invited people to put prayer requests in a basket that the pastor then placed on the altar with a prayer. Lindy asked Grandma, "Now what happens?"

"We've put our requests before God, Lindy, just like we put a cake in the oven. We turn on our faith, leave our requests on the altar, and now we must *let God do His work*. He knows how long His perfect answer will take."

TRUST GOD TO DO HIS WORK IN HIS TIMING . . . FOR AS LONG AS IT TAKES FOR HIS PERFECT RESULT!

THE SLOW TRACK

Commit your way to the LORD;
trust in Him, and He will act,
making your righteousness shine like the dawn,
your justice like the noonday.

(PSALM 37:5–6)

The accident wasn't Emmit's fault. A large truck had run a red light and hit him broadside while he was riding his motorcycle. Those who saw the accident thought it was a miracle Emmit survived, and without brain damage. His left leg, however, had been shattered. He faced months of surgeries and rehab.

All of this was highly discouraging to Emmit, who was not known for his patience.

A friend from church came to visit Emmit, and Emmit opened up to him. "I figured God wanted me to be an example of one of His *big* miracles. But frankly, I'm frustrated that God didn't heal me *immediately*. What's the purpose of this long, slow, painful process?" He finally sighed and said, "This accident is a *stop* sign in my life."

Robert listened patiently and then said, "Maybe it's a *yield* sign."

"Yield what?" Emmit asked. "I know God is going to heal me and my leg is going to be as good as new. Why not speed up the process? I'm ready for fast forward!"

Robert replied, "It might be a lesson—not just for you but for lots of other people—about your trust in God to do things *His* way and in *His* timing."

"What are you suggesting?" Emmit asked sincerely.

"Let's pray and ask God to show you *why* He has you on this long, slow healing journey. Ask Him to let you see your nurses, rehab helpers, and the other patients in rehab in a new light. Maybe there's something you are to say to them about God. The slow process just may be for the people around you to reach the point of being able to trust you and really hear what you say. God may have you on the slow track for *their* sake."

God uses SLOW for His purposes.

Faith to Let Go

I trust in God's faithful love forever and ever.

(Psalm 52:8)

*I*t was near dusk when Paul found himself suddenly sliding downward out of control. He hadn't realized he was at the edge of a cliff—he hadn't even realized there was a cliff in the area!

Paul reached out and grabbed hold of a large root that had thrust through the side of the rocky cliff, and hung on for dear life. Slowly, he began to find some crevices for his feet and his other hand. His friend Ted called to him, "Hang on, Paul! Sam is going for help. I'll stay here. Be brave! Don't let go!"

Darkness fell and Paul struggled to stay awake and to keep his fingers from going numb as he clung tightly to the root and rocks. He struggled even more when he called out to his friend Ted and didn't get an answer—he felt angry at Ted for either falling asleep or leaving for comfortable shelter. Mostly, however, he felt sad, lonely, and frightened.

"God, are You up there?" he called. To his great surprise, Paul heard a deep, gentle voice reply, "Yes, I'm here."

"Help me!" Paul cried.

"Okay," the voice said. "Will you do what I tell you to do?"

"Oh, yes!" Paul said. The voice then said, "Let go."

Paul was stunned. He finally got out a reply, "Is there anybody else up there I can talk to?" Silence.

The rest of the night passed. Paul remained scared, and angry at his friends.

As morning began to dawn, Paul looked around him, and then looked *down*. He saw that he was just a few feet above a broad level area—a "platform" of sorts.

Paul "let go." And managed to get an hour of very deep sleep lying on the broad grassy ledge before his friends arrived with help.

LETTING GO IS OFTEN THE NECESSARY ACT OF FAITH.

THE SHORTEST LECTURE

With the faithful
You prove yourself faithful;
With the blameless man,
You prove yourself blameless.
(PSALM 18:25)

*E*very person in the jammed lecture hall was eager to hear what the wise old Bible teacher had to say. This particular teacher was long past retirement age, but each year, a group of students presented him with a petition begging him to teach just "one more year" so they could learn from him.

As the old professor walked to the lectern that morning, the students gave him a standing ovation. He smiled and motioned for them to take their seats.

"I'm an old man as you can see," he said with a twinkle in his eyes. "I don't know how many hours I have left on this earth, much less how many hours I might have to teach you this semester. So I'm going to start by telling you the most important thing I can say to you. Listen closely. I want you to take my words as a command straight from God."

The students were eager to comply. Notebooks flew open. Pens were poised.

"Take off your shoes," the professor said. Thinking they were preparing to stand on holy ground, the students quickly did as he commanded.

"Now on the bottom of your right shoe I want you to write in big, bold capital letters the word TRUST." The students looked at one another a bit stunned but did what he said.

"Now on the bottom of your left shoe I want you to write in similar letters the word OBEY." They did as he said.

"Now put your shoes back on. The Christian life boils down to TRUST and OBEY. I want you to get up and walk out of this lecture hall, and what you have written on your *soles*, I want you to write on your *souls*. Class dismissed."

To walk in faith, TRUST and OBEY.

From Where I Am . . .

He leads me along the right paths for His name's sake.

(Psalm 23:3)

A seminar leader asked the women attending to tell the greatest lesson they had learned in their childhood about faith. One woman told this story:

"I was excited about my first day of kindergarten. Two weeks before classes started, my mother and I toured my classroom and I met my teacher. Mom showed me where the buses dropped us off at the school. I could see my classroom from the drop-off point. It all seemed easy.

"I asked Mom, 'What if I get lost?' Mom replied, 'Jesus always knows where you are. He knows how to get you from where you are to where you need to be.'

"Well, when we arrived on the bus that first day, a teacher was guiding all of the children to the *left*, not to the *right* where I could see my classroom. I protested but the teacher pointed sternly that I was to follow the river of children going to the *left*. I was in a near panic. I had no idea where I was, where I was going, or how to get to my classroom. All of the other students seemed older and very confident. I fought back tears.

"Then I remembered Mom's words. I whispered, 'Jesus, You know where I am. You know how to get me from where I am to where I need to be.' And I kept walking. Pretty soon, the river of children became a stream, and then—up ahead, I could see my kindergarten teacher standing outside my classroom. I had made it!

"That prayer my mother taught me when I was five years old is one I pray often: 'Jesus, You know where I'm at. You know how to get me from where I am to where You want me to be!'"

TRUST JESUS TO GUIDE YOU TO WHERE
HE WANTS YOU TO BE.

NECESSITIES

[Jesus said,] "Your Father knows the things
you need before you ask Him."
(MATTHEW 6:8)

On an early morning run to the grocery store, a woman smiled as she saw a man emerge from the store with an armful of frozen dinners in one hand and a package of twelve rolls of toilet tissue in the other. "His *necessities*," she thought, as she giggled to herself.

The man in line right before her at the checkout station had in his cart a large package of disposable baby diapers and about twenty assorted jars of baby food. *Necessities!*

The woman behind her in line? Two boxes of facial tissue and a bottle of cold medicine.

Necessities!

Her own *necessities* that day? Coffee creamer and a bouquet of flowers for a friend's birthday luncheon.

As she mused on the idea of necessities, she recalled the words of a wise older friend who had once noted ruefully, "Every family always seems to be out of *something*—usually just one thing, pretty much all the time. Even if an 'emergency supply' is purchased and stashed away, that supply always seems to be consumed before it is replaced!"

What about our needs, and our faith? Do we find ourselves repeatedly "a quart low on faith" for the same need, again and again . . . and again? Does a particular type of need always seem to smack us on our blind side, demanding that we believe *yet once again* for the same miracle or supply of provision?

What are you believing God to do today? Is it something about which you *repeatedly* find yourself trusting God?

Ask the Lord today to help you put in place a combination of spiritual disciplines, advance warning signals, and practical help that will fuel your faith so that you have a more-than-ample supply when your particular brand of need rears its ugly head!

FAITH IS NOT A LUXURY—IT IS A NECESSITY!

Rise and Make Up Your Bed

Peter said to him, "Aeneas, Jesus Christ heals you. Get up and make your bed," and immediately he got up.

(Acts 9:34)

The New Testament tells a brief story about a man named Aeneas, who was paralyzed and bedridden for eight years by the time the apostle Peter showed up at his house.

Peter declared to him, "Aeneas, Jesus the Christ heals you. Rise and make up your bed."

The Bible goes on to say, "Immediately he got up."

What an amazing miracle! Those who have been bedridden for a long time rarely have sufficient strength to lift their heads off a pillow, much less *get up*. And even if they are able to stand and walk, it is another feat of effort to *make up one's bed*.

Peter's words no doubt inspired tremendous faith to surge through Aeneas. But, it wasn't enough for Aeneas to *believe* the truth proclaimed by Peter. Aeneas was challenged to *act* on what he believed.

To "rise" meant to make an effort that was in defiance of his need. It meant exerting himself toward a new goal.

To "make up his bed" meant intentionally setting in place a barrier to his returning to his pallet. It meant adopting a new set of habits and a new level of self-responsibility.

If you are stuck today in a paralyzing pattern—perhaps in your body, in a relationship, in your finances, or in your career—accept and act on the truth that

- the Lord desires to help you regain full mobility, energy, and fulfilling purpose;
- the Lord asks that you do something to counteract the paralysis;
- the Lord wants you to choose new attitudes, disciplines, and goals that will enable you to move forward . . . and upward!

Faith is trusting God to help you do what you can do—even as you trust Him to do on your behalf what you cannot do.

TODAY, DO SOMETHING PRACTICAL AND
CONCRETE AS AN ACT OF YOUR FAITH.

AS THEY WERE GOING

While they were going,
they were healed.
(LUKE 17:14)

*L*eprosy was greatly feared in Bible times. The word "leprosy" was used for a number of skin conditions—including psoriasis, hives, and boils. Those afflicted with leprosy faced a prognosis of ongoing pain and increasing physical limitations. Lepers were ostracized from society and could have no physical contact with anyone other than fellow lepers. Many towns in ancient Israel had a small group of lepers living on their outskirts.

Family members who brought food and other necessities to their loved ones with leprosy had to stand many yards away from them, rarely getting close enough to look in their eyes. As a result, lepers felt little compassion from the ones they loved the most. The Law prohibited lepers from engaging in any religious ceremonies, so a dimension of faith was also stripped from them.

Should a person's skin condition improve, a leper could only be restored to society after a priest had examined the person and pronounced him "clean."

One day as Jesus neared a village, a group of lepers called to Him from a distance, "Jesus, Master, have mercy on us!"

Jesus called back, "Go, and show yourselves to the priests." They took His words as a command of healing, and the Bible tells us, *"As they were going* they were cleansed." They started out toward the priests as lepers. They arrived as men with clear skin!

These men believed what Jesus commanded more than they believed the outward visible circumstance of their lives. They trusted Jesus to heal and restore more than they believed leprosy to continue.

Are you believing today for a bad status quo to continue or for things to get worse? Or, are you willing to hear and obey what Jesus tells you to do that is related to your total healing—spirit, mind, and body?

SEE YOURSELF AS WALKING INTO
THE MIRACLE YOU NEED!

FAITH GOALS

"Look with your eyes, listen with your ears, and pay attention to everything I am going to show you."

(EZEKIEL 40:4)

*D*o you have personal faith goals?

Are you trusting God for something specific?

Have you set goals that you know you can reach *only* with God's help?

A pastor recently challenged his congregation to set "faith goals" rather than make New Year's resolutions. "Resolutions tend to last about a month," he noted. "Everybody makes the same resolutions to lose weight, get fit, pay down their debt, and stop their worst habit. When people fail at resolutions, they feel guilty . . . and then, life goes on.

"I'm challenging you to go to God and ask what *He* wants to do in or through you during the coming year. It may be just one thing, or several. What *He* wants will always have the potential for eternal rewards.

"And then, commit yourself to doing what God wants. Pray, 'I need Your help, Lord. I'm trusting and believing *You* are in this with me!'

"Put God in the driver's seat. Make a decision that you will trust Him daily to lead you one step closer to the goal He has set *with* you for your life."

At the end of the year, three people reported at the church's annual meeting:

- "I'll never make another resolution again. I'll *only* make faith goals. They work."
- "I felt God leading me to set a faith goal in two important areas of my life. I acted on those goals every day with my faith. Life took on a whole new glow!"
- "I had never thought about spiritual growth and change in terms of a faith goal. I will never try to change something again without God first confirming to me that He wants the change, and then, relying on Him daily for help."

WHAT ARE YOU BELIEVING GOD DESIRES FOR YOU?

FINDING THE FULCRUM

We have this hope as an anchor for our lives, safe and secure.
(HEBREWS 6:19)

A woman and her friend were excited about leaving their university studies in England for a fall break excursion to Paris. They eagerly boarded a large ferry in Southampton for their crossing of the English Channel. The skies were clear and the sea calm as they began their voyage.

Things changed dramatically as they neared the halfway mark in the channel. The sea began to churn, sending the boat pitching violently.

One of the woman remained in the back of the boat and quickly became nauseous to the point where she could not move from her seat. The other woman forced herself to get up and move forward. A strange idea kept coming to mind, "Find the fulcrum."

She later said, "I must have learned the word 'fulcrum' in high school. It certainly wasn't a concept I had ever thought about using before that day!"

A fulcrum, of course, is the point at which a lever turns. Although the ferry was acting like a bucking bronco, the degree of motion at the midway point of the boat was remarkably calm. In the seat this young woman found at the fulcrum, she was able to relax and begin to imagine that she was being gently rocked in the arms of God her loving Father, as if she were a baby.

In a world that seems out of control on all sides, in a world that is causing you to be sick and unsettled in your soul, ask the Lord to show you the fulcrum in your life and to help you see Him as the One who will not only bring you through the difficult times, but will comfort you with His presence as you make life's voyage.

FAITH SEARCHES OUT THE FULCRUM OF GOD'S LOVE.

One Foggy Night

Faith is the reality of what is hoped for,
the proof of what is not seen.
(Hebrews 11:1)

*T*hose who live in the central San Joaquin Valley of California know that, on occasion, fog can become so thick that visibility nears zero. Airplanes are grounded. Driving is hazardous.

Such fog can roll in quickly, and that is what happened one night as a family of four began to make their way home from an evening church event twenty miles from their small town.

They needed to travel twelve miles by freeway and then another six miles on a four-lane divided road, plus two miles of city streets. It all seemed fairly straightforward. The trip normally took twenty minutes. That night, it took two hours!

"We could only see one hash mark on the freeway concrete," the daughter of the family later recounted. "We were all praying that God would show us the exit from the freeway. That was the critical point."

"Were you scared?" a friend asked.

"At the beginning we were. Mostly we were afraid of being hit by a driver who wasn't as cautious as Dad, or of hitting a vehicle that had stopped at the side of the road. But then, as we traveled mile after mile, we relaxed and saw our trip as a big faith adventure. We each had a deep belief that God was with us, leading us minute by minute in the right way to go, even though we could see *nothing*."

Those who walk by faith gain a track record of experience—they find it easier to trust God in an emergency, even if they cannot see a way out of a dire circumstance. "We didn't need to see the way fully," this young woman concluded. "We were trusting the One who *could* see through the fog and who could see us on the road."

TRUST GOD—HE CAN SEE WHAT YOU CANNOT.

A Bit at a Time

The LORD will provide what is good.

(PSALM 85:12)

The surgery had seemed routine . . . until a staph infection set in. Now Cynthia had been in the hospital for three months and there was no release date in sight. The infection had gone, but a follow-up surgery was necessary for some skin grafts.

"I thought I had a firm faith," Cynthia said to her friend Gloria, who had come to the hospital over her noon hour for a visit. "Now, I'm starting to wonder. It seems to me that if I just had a better faith—or maybe a bigger faith or a stronger faith—that I could get past this infection and see my skin healed so I wouldn't need more surgery. I'm so eager to get back home and get on with my life!"

"It's about one o'clock in the afternoon. How much faith do you need for the rest of today?" Gloria asked, looking at her watch to illustrate her question.

"What do you mean?" Cynthia asked.

"What are you facing this afternoon? And, how much faith do you need to trust God to help you face it?"

"Well, they are changing my dressings, and that's always painful. I need faith to beat the pain."

"Let's pray for that!" Gloria said. After they prayed, Cynthia said, "I get your point, Glo. God isn't expecting me to come up with a big lump of faith to solve my entire problem—He wants me to muster the faith I need to take the next small step."

"A bit of faith . . . a bit of progress . . . a bit more healing!" said Gloria.

"A bit of faith" became Cynthia's goal. She told her friend later, "For each step, God seems to give me just enough faith to take that step. One step forward every day—that's progress!"

FAITH SOMETIMES WORKS BEST IN BIT-SIZED PORTIONS.

A Different Team?

*Encourage one another and build each other
up as you are already doing.*
(1 Thessalonians 5:11)

Timmy could hardly believe the score: 10 to 0! His team had won again, the third time in three weeks! In fact, they had a "winning season" in the bag since there were only two games left.

"It's so much *fun* to win!" Timmy said to his dad as he climbed into the back seat of their SUV.

Timmy loved all the high-fives, the cheers from the stands, and the look of satisfaction on the coach's face.

"Quite a change from last year, isn't it?" Dad said.

"Sure is!" Timmy didn't really enjoy thinking about last year. The team had lost *all* of its games the previous season, some of them by embarrassingly large margins. He hadn't been tempted to quit the team, but he knew that some of his teammates had felt that way.

Timmy wasn't the star of the team. In fact, he wasn't even a player. He was the "water boy," officially called the "trainer's assistant." Timmy had a physical limitation that kept him from playing at the level required, but he had no less love for the game or enthusiasm for his teammates. The other members of the team treated him as if he was fully a part of them, and had even insisted that the coach give

Timmy a uniform and a number. For his part, Timmy not only helped the team in any practical way he could, but he was their number-one cheerleader and encourager.

"What do you think has made the difference between this year and last year?" Dad asked as they drove home.

Without any hesitation, Timmy replied with enthusiasm, "This year they started *believing* me when I told them they could *win*!"

Are you believing today what God says to you about your potential, His help, and your ability to *win*?

PLAY LIKE YOU ARE ON GOD'S WINNING TEAM!

Upstream Paddling

"I have seen his ways,
but I will heal him;
I will lead him and restore comfort
to him and his mourners,
creating words of praise."

(Isaiah 57:18–19)

*B*renda and her father were glad to be on a canoe float trip with several other father-daughter teams from their church. The river near their town had only a few rapids and no major rock outcroppings. Because they were both experienced canoers, Brenda and Dad were asked to bring up the rear of their "canoe caravan." That way they could help any canoers who ran into trouble on the river. They were honored to take on that role.

Everything about the day seemed to be perfect for a relaxed afternoon on the water. The scenery was beautiful and the weather was warm . . . and then without any apparent cause, Brenda's left oar slide through her fingers *and* through its guide.

Dad reacted quickly. "Turn around and let's paddle back to get it!" They both quickly reversed their positions and began to paddle upstream to where they could see the oar lodged in some tall reeds near the river's edge.

Once the oar had been retrieved and they were again headed downstream, Brenda realized they were both huffing and puffing. "Whew!" she exclaimed. "That was harder than I anticipated! We only paddled about fifty yards and we are soaked with perspiration. The current is stronger than I thought."

"Right!" Dad agreed. "Just goes to prove once again that paddling *upstream* is an entirely different experience that paddling *downstream*. Downstream is guiding, upstream is *work*."

The faith challenges that come during hard times can be intense. It often seems to take far more faith to *regain* something lost than to *maintain* something good. God's desire is always to keep us on a good course. We can trust Him to help us reverse (repent) when we need to, recover what is recoverable, and get back in the flow.

If God wants you to gain it, he'll help you if you need to regain it.

No Shifting

*Every generous act and every perfect gift is from above,
coming down from the Father of lights; with Him there
is no variation or shadow cast by turning.*

(James 1:17)

I'm glad God tells the truth," Sandi said to her mother as they were driving around town on errnds. The comment seemed to come out of nowhere and Sandi's mother was a bit surprised. "What brought about that profound statement?" she asked in a slightly teasing voice.

"Well, if God always tells the truth then I can count on things from God," Sandi said.

"Like what?" Mom asked.

"Well, when God says *not* to do something—or *else*—He means it. And when He says He loves us, He also means it. I don't have to wonder if God feels one way on one day and another way the next day. When God promises something, He'll *do it!*"

"What brought about this wonderful insight?" Mom asked, happy at Sandi's level of understanding. After all, Sandi was only eight years old.

"My Sunday school teacher had us memorize a verse last week that said, 'There is no shadow of turning in God.' None of us really knew what that meant so she told us."

"What *does* it mean?" Mom asked.

"It means God doesn't even change a *little bit* to cause a different shadow on the ground. The teacher had us all stand up and she turned on a bright light that caused us to have extra long shadows on the floor. Then she had us move, and when we did, we all saw that our shadows moved! That was cool. We could tell if a person moved even a little bit because their shadow moved.

"The teacher said, 'God never shifts in His seat on the throne of heaven! We can count on His being just who He says He is, and stay that way.'

"I *like* that," Sandi said.

"So do I!" Mom agreed.

TRUST GOD TODAY TO BE TRUE TO
HIS PROMISES TO YOU.

The West Bank at Midnight

I am teaching you the way of wisdom;
I am guiding you on straight paths.
(Proverbs 4:11)

group of four women once found themselves driving up the West Bank in Israel from Jericho to Tiberias. They had never planned to take that particular route and certainly hadn't counted on driving this road at night.

One woman in their tour group had become ill and needed assistance at Jerusalem's main hospital. Two women had stayed to be with her, and the fourth woman was the only one available to drive their standard-transmission rental car!

As they traveled north, they were stopped numerous times at military roadblocks. The Israeli soldiers were shocked to find four American women out alone in the darkness of the night. The women soon learned that all Israel was on high alert in anticipation of a possible invasion from Syria!

To compound matters, the women also discovered that the two-lane road had many dips, twists, potholes, and washed-out sections. The road was not marked with painted lines at the road edges, nor were there dividing marks between the lanes. Much of the asphalt was covered by sand.

One of the women commented, "I had heard about 'walking by faith' but never about 'driving by faith.'

"We may not have known where we were, or what we were going to encounter in the next five miles or next two hours," the driver of the car noted. "But we knew Who did know! We held on as our car bounced along. But mostly we held on to the Lord, the Author of our lives, and the Host of His homeland on this earth." She then added, "Is life any different? Most of the time we really don't know fully where we are, and especially in times of ups, downs, and potholes. But we know Who knows! And that's all that matters."

GOD KNOWS THE ROAD OF LIFE YOU ARE TRAVELING
BETTER THAN YOU CAN EVER KNOW IT!

NOTHING . . . OR EVERYTHING

Casting all your care on Him, because He cares about you.
(1 PETER 5:7)

*H*e can't do nuthin'," Harry, age five, said with a high degree
of disgust in his voice. He had hoped for a little brother who
could run and play and have fun with him. The newborn lying in the
crib before him was a huge disappointment.

"He can't do *anything,*" Mom said, correcting Harry's vocabulary.

"Yeah, he can't do that either," Harry responded.

"Well, he *can* eat, sleep . . . ," Mom suggested.

"And he sure can burp and fill a diaper," Harry added with a laugh.

"Actually, Harry, the only things that little Nick can do are things
that will help him grow up so he *can* do all the things you want him
to do."

In truth, *none* of us can do anything of vital importance on our
own strength, no matter our age.

We cannot make our heart beat its next beat.

We cannot make our lungs take their next breath.

Jesus noted to His followers that they were incapable of increasing
their height or ensuring that they would live another day.

Although we *think* we can, we truly cannot determine our own
destiny, ensure our own financial future, go through life without

any setbacks or disappointments, or finish *anything*. As one woman pointed out, "There's always a little more laundry that *could* be done."

What we *can* do is make choices to obey God and trust Him to do for us what *only* He can do. We must trust God to provide for us, protect us, lead and guide us, forgive us, redeem us from sin's power, and prepare us to live with Him forever.

The truth is: The areas in which we can do "nuthin'" are the very areas in which God offers to do everything.

GOD ASKS US TO BE DEPENDENT ON HIM,
NOT INDEPENDENT FROM HIM.

HE HASN'T MOVED

Trust in the LORD forever,
because in Yah, the LORD, is an everlasting rock!
(ISAIAH 26:4)

A man and wife found themselves stuck in freeway traffic. An accident had blocked all lanes, and a radio announcer informed them they could expect at least an hour delay.

The wife said, "Do you remember when this happened to us shortly after we had started dating?" The man nodded. She continued, "We weren't the least bit upset. It meant another hour we could be together—just the two of us shielded from all the world, with nothing else pulling at our attention or demanding our time." He smiled.

"I remember that old car," the wife went on, "with its bench-style front seat. There was no law about wearing seat belts back then, remember?" The man nodded and smiled. "We sometimes snuggled so close that people driving behind us couldn't tell there was more than one person in the car!"

The woman sighed deeply as she looked at the immobile lanes of traffic on both sides of them. "And now look at us. We're stuck on this freeway feeling frustrated and tense that we are losing valuable time and wasting gas. You can barely reach my hand to pat it, much less put your arm around me and hold me close."

After a few moments of silence the husband spoke softly, "I haven't moved."

How many times in life do you find yourself feeling hurried and harried, and in the process, distant from God? Do you find yourself wondering if God cares, if He is available to you, if He is *present*?

The truth is, God hasn't moved! He'd love for you to move closer to Him and trust Him to be with you, help you, communicate with you, and encourage you every moment of your day's journey. Relax, and by faith, move closer to Him.

TAKE ANY DELAY AS AN OPPORTUNITY TO DEEPEN
YOUR RELATIONSHIP WITH THE LORD.

SLEEPING LIKE A BABY

*You will keep the mind that is dependent on You
in perfect peace, for it is trusting in You.*
(ISAIAH 26:3)

"Don't you wish you could sleep like they do?" Ginny asked her friend Jill. The two young women were out for an afternoon walk with their six-month-old babies in their strollers . . . fast asleep.

"A full tummy, a clean diaper, and a little sunshine. What more could a baby ask for!" Jill responded.

"And isn't it amazing," Ginny continued, "they can fall asleep in a noisy mall just as quickly as out here in the fresh air. They can be in a room full of adoring and noisy adults, and suddenly develop those sleepy eyes, and *wham*, they're out."

"I think it has to do with more than biorhythms and daily schedules," Jill said. "I think it has to do with the fact that neither one of our babies has ever experienced real *fear*. At least not in a way that was identifiable to them as fear."

"You may be onto something there," Ginny said. "Our babies both were delivered surgically so they don't even have the innate fear of falling that many doctors say is the most basic of all fears."

"Can you even *imagine* what it might be like to have no fear whatsoever . . . never have *had* fear . . . none at all about anything?" Jill asked.

"No fear of not being able to be a good mother. No fear of not being able to pay this month's bills. No fear of sickness or death," Ginny offered.

"No fear of being assaulted or robbed," Jill picked up the theme. "No fear of being rejected or ridiculed. No fear of failure or war."

"It sounds like . . . "

"*Heaven!*" both young women said at the same time.

"And until we get there," concluded Jill, "a good night's sleep."

U<small>SE YOUR FAITH TO DEFEAT YOUR FEARS.</small>

THE LUMBERJACK

*"For I know the plans I have for you"—this is the Lord's
declaration—"plans for your welfare, not for disaster."*
(JEREMIAH 29:11)

lumberjack working in an enchanted forest was assigned by the
forest king to cut down one tree a day and turn it into wood
pieces. These, in turn, were delivered to the people of his village to
use for building or for burning in their stoves to heat their homes and
cook their food.

The lumberjack enjoyed his work, but one day he noted that every
morning, a new tree appeared in the forest. At first, he was pleased
with this. But then the thought occurred, *I'm never going to finish this
work.* The idea was depressing and the next day, he stayed home. And
the next, and the next.

Nobody noticed for a while, but then the villagers began asking
about their dwindling supply of wood. He responded with negative
words about the difficulty of his job and its futility.

After a few *weeks*, the lumberjack noticed that he lost all of his
strength and energy.

The lumberjack went to see the king about assigning him to a
different job. "I gave you the strength and ability to be a lumberjack,"
the king said. "I gave you a job you did well. I didn't ask you to clear

the forest. I asked only that you do what was for your benefit and that of your neighbors."

The lumberjack went home to think about what the forest king had said. And the next day . . . he wisely picked up his axe and returned to the forest!

TRUST GOD TO GIVE YOU THE WORK THAT IS BEST FOR YOU TO DO—AND STICK WITH IT.

FACTORED IN

Trust in Him at all times.

(PSALM 62:8)

*A*n old steam engine train was huffing and puffing its way through the countryside when it suddenly ground to a halt. The only passenger in the three-car train got up quickly and hurried to find the conductor. "What has happened?" he asked in a demanding voice. "I have a very important appointment in the next town and I must not be late. Surely this old train can make it through a flat pasture!"

The conductor smiled and nodded. "Nothing to worry about, sir. There's a cow on the tracks. She'll move on in a minute. We just have to wait her out."

For the next ten minutes, the angry man repeatedly consulted his watch as he fidgeted in his seat. Finally the train lurched forward . . . only to stop again after several miles.

This time the conductor came to the man and said, "Don't worry. We'll be on our way shortly." The man replied, "Did that cow catch up with us?" The conductor laughed heartily, but the businessman was far from even smiling.

To his absolute amazement, the train pulled into the town that was the man's destination five minutes before its scheduled arrival.

"Astonishing!" he said to the conductor. "I cannot believe we aren't late."

"Never are," said the conductor. And then he added, "The folks who made up the schedule allowed for delays caused by cows on the track."

If you are frustrated by delays today—perhaps appointments that show up late, freeways jammed with traffic, breakdowns in equipment—recognize that God is in charge of all things. He knew your schedule before you ever set foot out the door of your home. Trust Him to give you the patience and grace to *enjoy* the journey, even as He helps you meet your goals.

TRUST GOD TO PROVIDE THE TIME YOU NEED TO
GET DONE WHAT HE HAS ASSIGNED YOU TO DO.

GOING WITH GOD

With God we will perform valiantly.

(PSALM 60:12)

A young ensign was nearing the completion of his first overseas tour of sea duty when he was given a rare opportunity to assume responsibility for getting the ship out of the port and headed toward open seas. He eagerly rose to the challenge!

With a series of crisp commands, he had all hands scurrying on deck, and very quickly the ship pulled away from the dock and entered the channel headed for the ocean. The entire ship was abuzz when word came that the crew had set a new record in getting the destroyer under way. The ensign glowed with pride.

The ensign was not surprised, therefore, when a fellow seaman came to him with a message from the captain. He was sure it would be a congratulatory note. To his surprise, however, he noted that it was a *radio* message. And that surprise turned to shock when he read these words:

"My personal congratulations upon completing your underway preparation exercise according to the book and with amazing speed. In your haste, however, you have overlooked one of the unwritten rules—make sure the captain is aboard before getting under way."

Often in our haste to do good, we make our plans and execute them without asking God about *His* timing. We seem especially prone to doing this when we are assured that we are doing what the Lord has asked us to do. We take the attitude, *Surely if God wants this, He wants me to do it NOW.* The greater truth is that every job and every mission has a precise "right timing" on God's calendar and clock.

Never assume that God is "along for the good ride" that you have engineered. Rather, ask that *you* be on board with the ride He has planned.

Don't ask God to go with you. Ask
for permission to go with Him.

PERSEVERING IN GOD'S ANSWERS

Hide me from the scheming of wicked people,
from the mob of evildoers,
who sharpen their tongue like swords
and aim bitter words like arrows.

(PSALM 64:2–3)

In 1982, a young internal-medicine resident, Barry Marshall, took a research interest in the cause of stomach ulcers. At that time most physicians believed that ulcers occurred in persons with a weak stomach lining, which made them more susceptible to excess acid and other harsh stomach "juices." Few remedies worked reliably.

One day while studying a stomach bipsy, Marshall saw organisms that resembled *Campylobacter* bacteria, a finding confirmed by pathologist J. Robin Warren. Marshall convinced Dr. Warren to join him in a study of one hundred ulcer patients over the next year. They found *Campylobacter* organisms in 87 percent of the cases they studied!

Several leading ulcer specialists dismissed their findings, however, claiming the bacteria grew on the specimens *after* the tissues were removed from the patients. For their part, Marshall and Warren stood by their findings and moved to the next step. They contended that if, indeed, bacteria was causing the ulcers, a known treatment for killing the bacteria should work. They gave their ulcer patients a combination of bismuth and antibiotics. Sure enough, ulcers began to be healed in record time!

Again, their reports met with skepticism. But Marshall persevered, reporting repeated studies until finally clinical trials were approved four years after his first report. The studies confirmed that bacteria not only can but often does cause ulceration.

Have you ever been firmly convinced that God has spoken to you His truth about a matter, only to have others dismiss or even ridicule your belief? Have you ever backed away from a "faith decision" because others told you that you were naïve, misinformed, or misguided?

Revisit what God has said. Confirm it as truth in God's Word. Then persevere.

If God said it, and you persevere in believing and doing it, then God will bring it to pass!

ENDURE IN YOUR BELIEVING!

Miracles, Not Magic

I will be with you—this is the Lord's declaration.

(Jeremiah 30:11)

During World War II, a young soldier fighting in Italy managed to jump into a foxhole just ahead of a spray of enemy bullets. He immediately began to claw frantically at the dirt to deepen the hole so he might have more protection against the continuing barrage of enemy fire.

As he scraped at the dirt with his hands, he unearthed a silver crucifix on a broken chain, an object no doubt left by a previous occupant of the foxhole.

Moments later, a figure leaped into the foxhole next to him.

As shells continued to scream just inches above their heads, the soldier turned to see that his new companion was an army chaplain. He held out the crucifix toward the chaplain and cried, "Am I glad to see you! How do you work this thing?"

In times of crisis, our first tendency is often to look for some sort of "magical solution" that will erase our need completely. It might be a medicine that we hope will be a "magic bullet" against the disease we are battling. It might be a lottery ticket that seems to hold out hope of riches to counteract the financial disaster we are facing. It might be a religious symbol that we hope will ward off any evil spirits that we suspect might be the cause of our woe.

God's Word challenges us to lay aside all "magic" and turn to God with simple trust, saying, "Lord, I acknowledge You as my Healer and Deliverer. I am trusting You for the miracle I need. I ask You to do Your work using whatever methods You want to use, in whatever sequence of timing."

Magic is rooted in illusion. Genuine miracles are rooted in sincere faith.

GOD KNOWS PRECISELY HOW TO
RESOLVE YOUR PROBLEM.

THIRTY-FOUR YEARS

Indeed, the LORD's hand is not too short to save,
and His ear is not too deaf to hear.

(ISAIAH 59:1)

Martha and Jeanne were meeting for their regular Thursday afternoon early supper at the extended care complex where they both lived. They always looked forward to their weekly time together—it was usually a time for sharing the happy events of the previous week, which always seemed to be filled with family, friends, and unusual outings. At times it was an evening for sharing concerns and spending a few minutes in prayer.

"Well," said Martha after they had decided on their meal choices, "it only took thirty-four years."

"What took thirty-four?" Jeanne asked.

"My young friend Rachel visited me. She confessed to me something I've known for years and years. She had only been *pretending* to be a Christian. She had never really surrendered her life and will to Christ Jesus. Because her father was a minister, she knew all the words to say and the right things to do, but in her heart she had hated God and didn't believe in or want anything to do with Jesus."

"Is Rachel your young friend who was abused by her uncle and shunned by her mother?"

"Yes," said Martha. "I knew she had some good reasons for being angry, but I also knew that God could soften her heart. I just wasn't sure I'd live to see the day."

Martha continued with a brightened glow, "But I did! Rachel told me she had accepted Jesus as her personal Savior three weeks ago. She is like a completely new person—and she sure has given me a boost in my faith. God may not act as quickly as I'd like at times, but this last week I got a good reminder that He is *always* at work! It took thirty-four years but I didn't give up, and neither did God."

DON'T BE DISCOURAGED IF GOD HASN'T
ANSWERED YOUR PRAYERS . . . YET.

FAITH FOR RIGHT NOW

*The righteous one rejoices in the L*ORD
and takes refuge in Him;
all those who are upright in heart will offer praise.
(PSALM 64:10)

Some people seem to believe that they are "too young" to exhibit great wisdom or excellence. The truth is, there is no magic age when genius manifests—there is no "maturity" required for great ideas to be started or expanded.

Benjamin Franklin was twenty-six when he wrote *Poor Richard's Almanac.* Isaac Newton was twenty-four when he presented the "law of gravitation." Charles Dickens was twenty-four when he first published *Pickwick Papers* and twenty-five when he wrote *Oliver Twist.* Thomas Jefferson was thirty-three when he drafted the Declaration of Independence.

Others seem to believe they are too "old" to be creative or technologically innovative. Verdi was eighty when he composed *Falstaff* and eighty-five when he wrote *Ave Maria.* Goethe was eighty when he wrote *Faust.* Tennyson was eighty when he wrote "Crossing the Bar." Michelangelo completed his greatest art at age eighty-seven. Grandma Moses was in her seventies when she began to paint. "The Colonel" was sixty-five when he began franchising his famous Kentucky-fried chicken. There is no age when ingenuity dissipates.

Still others seem to believe that dementia is a "given" and that the brain cannot continue to produce brilliant ideas after a certain age. Justice Holmes was still writing Supreme Court opinions at age ninety. Immanuel Kant wrote his finest philosophical works at age seventy-four. There is no set age when inspiration or mental ability automatically declines.

Never think you are too young to produce something life-impacting or eternity-changing. Never think time has passed you by when it comes to your ability to create or invent something highly influential. Never allow your own self-value to diminish or to think yourself "irrelevant."

Do what you know to do to stay healthy in body, mind, and spirit. And then, trust God to help you express your highest and best right *now*.

TRUST GOD TO HELP YOU "MAX OUT"
YOUR CURRENT POTENTIAL!

God's Property

"I will now rise up," says the Lord. *"I will put
the one who longs for it in a safe place."*

(Psalm 12:5)

A young coed was walking across campus late one night. Even
though the area was fairly well lit, she suddenly realized that
she was alone. And then, from the shadows of a nearby building, a
figure came running to her, grabbed her by the hair, and pulled her
with him back into the shadows. She saw the glint of a knife and soon
felt its cold blade against her throat.

"Do what I say and I won't kill you," the voice said.

The young woman replied with loud voice and measured boldness,
"Take your hands off me. I am God's property."

"Oh?" he sneered in derision. "Right now, missy, you are
my property."

She countered, "No, I am not. I believe in Jesus and that makes me
His property."

To this day she cannot explain what happened next. The man
dropped the knife and ran away from her as fast as he could. The knife
left behind had fingerprints, of course, and they led to his identification
and arrest within a matter of days. He was a convicted rapist who
had just been released from prison the day before his confrontation

with this young woman—after serving ten years of hard time in the state penitentiary.

In sharing her story with university officials, she said, "I truly don't know what gave me the boldness to say what I said. All I knew is that I *had* to speak up and speak the *truth*—and the truth is, every person who believes in Jesus becomes fully God's property and God's responsibility."

Whose property are you? If you belong to God, then the greater question for your day is this:

What are you trusting God to do for you, in you, and through you?

Live as God's property on loan to

the world for good works!

STAY CONNECTED

I keep the LORD in mind always,
Because He is at my right hand,
I will not be shaken.
(PSALM 16:8)

*N*othing can derail a person's faith or sabotage a person's effectiveness as quickly or completely as uncontrolled anger. Anger is a God-given emotion, but the *purpose* for anger is often misunderstood. Anger has been given to mankind to motivate a person to seek justice or to right a wrong. For that to happen, anger must be focused and its emotional energy must be used in a positive way toward a positive goal.

"Fly off the handle" is a phrase commonly used to describe out-of-control anger. What an appropriate metaphor! The phrase originally referred to the head of a hammer becoming disconnected while a carpenter was in the process of working.

A disconnected hammer head rendered the hammer useless. It created a potentially dangerous and damaging situation—no one can predict where a flying hammerhead might land! Plus, the repair of the hammer, or the gaining of its replacement, interrupts the workflow and slows progress.

The same things happen when anger is misappropriated. The person displaying out-of-control anger is rarely taken seriously, much less admired or respected. The angry person wounds others with his words, and if the anger is habitual, the wounds can take on the nature of emotional abuse. Contrary to a popular saying, words *can hurt* as much as sticks and stones. Anger keeps a positive relationship from growing, and can even signal the end of a relationship. In all, there is far more to be lost by anger than there is to be gained.

Finally, anger is an indication that a person is not trusting God—either in a relationship or for God to work in the other person's life. If anger is a mark of your life, trust God to help you control your anger and use it for godly outcomes.

Keep your temperament and your faith connected!

YOU ARE THE BEST THERMOSTAT OF YOUR
OWN EMOTIONAL TEMPERATURE.

A Bazillionth Chance

[Jesus said,] "The Son of Man has come to seek and to save the lost."
(Luke 19:10)

Marilyn felt drawn to a young woman who remained in a pew after a church service had ended. Nearly everyone else had left the nave. She saw that the woman had her head down, and tears were flowing freely into her lap.

Marilyn entered the pew and sat next to her in silence. The young woman didn't move and didn't attempt to stop crying. Marilyn took this as a sign that the woman welcomed her presence, and after a few minutes, she reached over and gently took the young woman's hand that was resting on the cushion between them. Again, the woman did not resist. Her tears continued.

Marilyn finally said softly as a prayer, "Jesus, help us. Please help us right now."

At this the woman sobbed, "Jesus might help you, but He won't help me."

"Oh?" Marilyn asked gently. "Well, if He helps me and I'm holding your hand, His help will be for both of us."

The young woman again sobbed, "I've done too many bad things. I've messed up too many times. I've used up all of my chances for God to forgive me."

Marilyn said, "Oh my dear, I have such good news. Do you see the cross up there on the altar? Well, I checked behind that altar just this morning and Jesus had put there a big new supply of chances. The note on the delivery form said they were to be used by those who needed a bazillionth new chance. Let's grab one right now."

The woman giggled—not loudly, but it was enough. She welcomed Marilyn's prayer for her and then said, "Jesus, I need a bazillionth chance. Please forgive me."

Marilyn said an amen that was loud enough for both of them.

IF YOU NEED GOD TO GIVE YOU A FRESH START AND
A BIG DOSE OF FORGIVENESS TODAY, JUST ASK!

A Divine Turnaround

We know that all things work together for
the good of those who love God.

(Romans 8:28)

Catherine Marshall, author of the international best seller *Christy*, did not always see herself as a successful author, or even as an obedient follower of Christ Jesus. After she had spent more than two years working on a manuscript she had titled *Gloria*, she abandoned the project, concluding that she had made a mistake in undertaking the project and perhaps had missed God's plan for those years.

Marshall went to a retreat house in Florida to sort out her feelings. While there, she reread a Bible story about a time when poisonous snakes began to fill the camp of the Israelites. The people recognized that the snakes were a punishment for their sin and they cried out to God. The Lord told Moses, their leader, to give this message to the people: "Make a snake image and mount it on a pole. When anyone who is bitten looks at it, he will recover" (Numbers 21:8).

As she reflected on this story, she suddenly realized that the Israelites were told to take what had hurt them badly and lift it up to God. In doing this, they were healed. So, too, she concluded, we each can take our mistakes and sins, lift them to God, and trust Him to heal us and forgive us. She wrote of her experience, "When any one of us has made a wrong (or even doubtful) turning in our lives through arrogance or lack of trust or impatience or fear—God will show us a way out."

No matter what we have done to get off the track of God's perfect plan for us, God knows a way to redeem the situation and restore our purpose. God doesn't have a "plan B." Rather, He always has a way of renewing "plan A"!

HAVE FAITH THAT GOD CAN AND DOES
RESTORE AND RENEW!

BACKSTAGE SUCCESS

[Jesus said,] "This is what
I command you: Love one another."
(JOHN 15:17)

$\mathcal{M}$any people think that faith can be used to achieve popularity or notoriety. They set themselves to *believe* they might become a famous actor or musician, or perhaps a famous politician, athlete, or prizewinner. Fame is elusive, however. Popularity is fickle. Those who seek fame often become disappointed. And often they become jealous of those who *are* famous.

Edmund Halley was certainly *worthy* of fame, but he didn't seek it. Halley had a colleague who did become immensely famous: Isaac Newton. Most people know about Newton's encounter with a falling apple and his eventual law of gravity. Newton revolutionized the study of astronomy.

It was Halley, however, who was behind the scenes—happily so. He challenged Newton to think through his original theories and he corrected his mathematical errors. He nagged Newton into writing his greatest work, *Mathematical Principles of Natural Philosophy*. Halley edited, supervised, and financed the book's publication, even though Newton had more money and could easily have paid the printing costs.

Newton almost immediately reaped great financial rewards that came from his fame. Halley received little credit. Halley did, however, use the principles Newton developed to predict the orbit of a comet that would later bear his name—Halley's Comet, which returns every seventy-six years. In his day, however, Halley lived without fame. He is considered one of the most selfless men in the history of science.

The Bible tells us that God is the One who raises people to a high profile. He is the One who puts people into "leadership," which is a biblical concept that includes fame and notoriety. His desire is *not* that we *aspire* to be famous but rather that we desire to *serve.* The servant who sees himself as "least" is often the person God elevates to "most."

TRUST GOD TO HELP YOU BE THE
SERVANT HE DESIRES YOU TO BE.

A FAMILY COMMITMENT

Fear the LORD and worship Him in sincerity and truth.

(JOSHUA 24:14)

As part of his farewell address to the Israelites, Joshua called upon the people to worship Jehovah only and obey His commandments completely.

He admonished the people to serve the Lord "in sincerity and truth." He wanted them to keep God's laws not only in their outward behavior but in their inward attitudes and desires. And even beyond that, to serve the Lord "in sincerity," which means to *want* to obey God. It is one thing to say and do the right thing in every situation, even to feel an obligation to do so. It is an entirely different level of commitment and trust to *want* to do what God desires!

Do you believe you *must* obey God? Or do you really *want* to live in close relationship with God and trust Him in every detail of your life? These questions go to the very nature of your faith.

Joshua went on to say, "As for me and my family, we will worship Yahweh" (Joshua 24:15). Two things are important to note:

First, Joshua didn't consider it enough that he had personally served and would continue to serve the Lord until the day he died. He wanted his faith to be the faith of every member in his household. As one man said about his family, "I don't intend to show up in heaven without my wife and children. It just wouldn't be heaven if they weren't there."

Second, in order to make this statement, Joshua likely had a prior conversation with his family. They no doubt had declared their individual desires to serve the Lord, with a *no matter what* commitment.

What about you and your family? Have you had a "talk" about your *family* commitment to trust God and serve Him? It's important to do so!

GOD LOVES YOU AND ALL THOSE YOU LOVE——
HE WANTS TO WELCOME YOUR FAMILY
INTO HIS ETERNAL PRESENCE.

FAMILY FAITH GOALS

"We will worship the LORD our God and obey Him."
(JOSHUA 24:24)

*W*hat are you and your family members, or perhaps a group of close friends, pursuing as your commonly shared "faith goals"?

A church recently challenged its families to set faith goals—as a family—rather than to make individual New Year's resolutions. "Get together and discuss what you are going to believe *together* for God to do in the coming year," the pastor said. "Go beyond what you each desire to change or see God do in your individual lives. Have a family goal that involves your faith! Set your hearts and minds on discovering what *God* wants you to be and do *as a family.*"

At the year's end, the pastor asked various ones to report about how their "faith goals" had worked out. Here is part of what was said:

- "In the past, our individual resolutions tended to fall by the wayside. Not so with our faith goals. They lasted all year."
- "We made getting out of family debt our primary faith goal. We agreed that if we could get out of debt as a family, we could do more for the Lord and also be more flexible in other areas of our lives. It meant a lot to have our teenagers on board with our free-of-debt goal."

- "We supported each other all year—reminding one another of our faith goals and praying together about them."
- "We added a motto to our list of three main faith goals: 'We're trustin' while we're truckin'.'"
- "We set family faith goals of working to feed the homeless, to pray for the church's missionaries every night, and to go on a summer mission to serve God. Our pursuit of those three goals has changed our lives forever."

Do you and your family have shared faith goals?

CALL A FAMILY MEETING AND SET
SOME MUTUAL FAITH GOALS!

FAITH TO STAND FIRM

*The priests carrying the ark continued standing in the
middle of the Jordan until everything was completed that
the Lord had commanded Joshua to tell the people.*

(JOSHUA 4:10)

*W*hen Dr. Frances Kelsey was named to the Federal Drug Administration in the 1960s, she was quickly inundated with work. At that time, the FDA was reviewing nearly seven hundred applications a year for the approval of new medicines, and the FDA had only sixty days to review each application before giving approval or requesting more data.

One of the applications that came across her desk was from a pharmaceutical firm in Ohio, which was applying for a license to market its drug called Kevadon. When taken in liquid form, the drug seemed to relieve nausea in early pregnancy. It had been given to millions of women, mostly in Europe, Asia, and Africa. Although the scientific data revealed potential negative side effects, the clinical reports from overseas confirmed that the drug did have amazing anti-nausea properties. The pharmaceutical firm had printed almost sixty-seven thousand leaflets declaring its safety—leaflets to be included in the boxes of the medicine once it was approved. The pressure on Dr. Kelsey was intense to give permission for labels to be printed and for the medicine to be approved for manufacturing.

Dr. Kelsey reviewed the data and said no. Through several rounds of applications, she continued to find the data "unsatisfactory." After fourteen months, the company withdrew its application. Why the change? Because Kevadon was *thalidomide,* and by that time, a flood of data had come in that the drug was responsible for deformities that included missing and stunted limbs in millions of babies. Dr. Kelsey's firm "no" spared untold agony in the United States.

Faith is used not only for saying "yes" to God's good plans, but also for saying "no" to those things that God prohibits or reveals as harmful.

A key question to ask *in faith* is, "Lord, is this something *You* want for me?"

GOD WANTS ONLY WHAT IS GOOD FOR YOU.

Go for the Perfect Fit

*Your eyes saw me when I was formless; all my days were written
in Your book and planned before a single one of them began.*

(PSALM 139:16)

The story is told of a boy who knew *exactly* what he wanted in
his future. He made a list and presented it to God. The list
included living in a big house with a garden . . . two Saint Bernard
dogs . . . a wife who was blue-eyed, tall, and beautiful . . . three sons—
one who would be a scientist, one a quarterback, and one a political
leader. Oh yes, and a red Ferrari!

The little boy had full confidence that God would give him all this,
and also help him to become a world-famous mountain climber.

As it turned out, the boy hurt his knee while playing football.
Mountain climbing was definitely out. He went on to college to
study business. He married a kind woman who was short and had
brown eyes. Because of his work, he lived in a big city, where he had
an apartment and the only garden nearby was a city park. He rode
subways and took cabs—and didn't own a car. He and his wife had
three daughters—one became a nurse, another a music teacher, and
the third an artist. They had a fluffy cat as their pet. One day the
man came across his list of boyhood ambitions. He had a momentary

attack of discouragement. "Those were all great dreams!" he cried out to God. "Why didn't You give me what I requested?"

He felt the Lord speak into his heart, "Because I wanted to give you what would truly make you joyful. I wanted to give you My best, for your best."

God knows who He has made you to be, and that includes what will fulfill you and deeply satisfy you. Trust Him to provide what fits His purpose for you.

PUT ON GOD'S PLANS FOR YOU—
THEY WILL FIT YOU PERFECTLY.

GOD BELIEVES IN YOU

We are His creation, created in Christ Jesus for good works, which
God prepared ahead of time so that we should walk in them.

(EPHESIANS 2:10)

Dad was doing his best to give a pep talk to his little ballerina, Kitty, age five.

"I'm scared," Kitty said as she waited with her father backstage at a ballet recital. A group of little girls was dancing on the stage, and Kitty's group was scheduled to go on stage next.

"Look at me," Dad said, insisting that Kitty lock into direct eye contact with him.

"I believe you can do this, Kitty. You are my brave, beautiful princess. I've seen you dance this dance at home and you do it very well. You have fun dancing. You like for Mom and me and your sister to have fun *watching* you dance. And I believe that you are going to go out there on that stage and show the people in the audience how much fun it is to dance! You don't have to be perfect. You just have to go out there and have fun. I *know* you *can* do this. I *believe* in you, Kitty!"

Dad talked until the previous group left the stage. "Now, give me a smile that says, *I believe you, Daddy!*" Kitty flashed a big smile at her father, went out on the stage, and danced with all her energy. When she rejoined him backstage after the dance, she had only three words to say, "That was *fun!*"

Long before you believed in God, He believed in you. He built into you just what it takes to do what He asks you to do. You are His beloved child and He delights in seeing you trust Him and take risks to share with others your relationship with Him. He believes you *can* do everything He has authorized you to do today!

GIVE GOD A SMILE TODAY AND GO OUT AND DANCE
THE DANCE HE HAS CHOREOGRAPHED FOR YOU!

MUTUAL EXPECTATION

[Jesus said,] "Consider the sower who went out to sow."
(MATTHEW 13:3)

Faith is often likened to a seed—ideally, a good seed planted in good soil, to produce something good in the world.

Noted Bible teacher D. L. Moody once said, "Very often you hear people say, 'The root of the matter is in him.' What would you say if I had a garden and nothing but roots in it?"

Seeds are *expected* to grow and produce a harvest. No farmer or gardener plants seeds expecting the seed to rot in the soil or to remain dormant there. No! The planter of seeds *expects* the seeds to germinate, sprout, and grow into a desired and profitable plant or tree that will yield a "crop" that is *greater* than the seed planted.

A farmer or gardener also knows that he has work to do once the planted seeds begin to grow. His job is cultivating, weeding, watering, fertilizing, and protecting the growing plants from creatures who would try to destroy them. He also must be vigilant in harvesting the crop at the right time—not too early, not too late.

At the same time, no farmer or gardener has the audacity to think that he or she can *cause* a seed to grow. The seed-sower knows his part is to do the planting of the best seed he has in the best soil he can find. Only God can *cause* a seed to grow. Only God can cause a seed to yield a harvest. Only God can *multiply* a seed into *more*.

God has faith in you that you can be a good sower and a good caretaker of a growing plant.

Believe in Him that He will cause what you plant in faith to grow and produce a harvest of blessing.

Mutual faith! Mutual expectation!

Do your part, and trust God to do His part!

11

VISIBILITY

What good is it, my brothers, if someone says
he has faith but does not have works?

(JAMES 2:14)

Mom peeked into the living room to find Tommy sitting silently at the piano. "Why aren't you practicing?" Mom said. "Why are you just sitting there?"

"I *am* practicing," Tommy said.

"Oh?" Mom said. "I don't hear any music."

"I'm practicing in my head," Tommy said. "I'm listening to the music in my mind."

"Hmmm," said Mom. "How does it sound?"

Tommy replied enthusiastically, "It's perfect! I'm not hitting any clunkers!"

"That's nice," Mom said. "I'm sure there must be some value in rehearsing the music in your mind."

Tommy beamed. Perhaps he had won his point!

"But," Mom continued, "I want to hear some practicing with your fingers on the keys. I want to hear the music with my ears that you are hearing in your brain. I don't mind hearing a few clunkers if I know you're on the way to playing without them!"

God's Word challenges us to have faith but then to *do* something with our faith that is visible, tangible, concrete, observable. "Show me your faith *by your works*," admonishes the book of James in the New Testament.

A basic principle in learning theory contends that a person learns a concept fully only in a process that involves the person being given "examples and non-examples." A student must see how an idea "plays out" in real life for the student to know how to apply an idea, how to test an idea, and how to develop an idea. The same goes for our faith. We need to put our faith to the test for our benefit and for the benefit of others who are in relationship with us.

How will others see that your faith works and that it is beneficial to life if you give them no examples?

TURN YOUR INNER FAITH INSIDE OUT!

BEING FAITH-FULL

*Hold on to the pattern of sound teaching that you have heard
from me, in the faith and love that are in Christ Jesus.*

(2 TIMOTHY 1:13)

I need to get some faith," Luke said.

"Why not just use the faith you've got?" his friend Sam replied.

The truth is, God's Word says you *have* a supply of faith as a gift from God (see Romans 12:3). What you *can* do is choose to acknowledge and activate your faith, and grow in your trust of God at all times and in all situations. You can choose to *endure* in faith.

Genuine faith has a persevering quality to it. In the Scriptures and in the writings of Christians through the ages, faith is nearly always linked to reliability, trustworthiness, and true "fidelity," which is often a synonym for unwavering loyalty.

The person of faith can be counted on to discharge his spiritual duties. He can be relied upon to pray quickly and earnestly for a person who has a need, and to persist in praying regardless of circumstances over time. He can be counted on to speak the truth of God's Word any time it is appropriate to do so, regardless of prevailing skepticism or doubt.

John M. Drescher wrote in his book *Spirit Fruit* that faith is "not the shrugging of the shoulders or a passive posture. Nor is it a 'grin and bear it' attitude. It is a positive, active attribute. It results from a love which keeps moving forward and comes out victorious. It remains steadfast and true in the midst of evil. The faithful person does not sidestep a situation or endeavor to escape to the easy path or flee when threats come. The faithful person stays at his station."

What a noble thing to have faith! What an enviable trait to be regarded as a person who is faithful, which might also be stated as "faith-*filled*." What an important role to *express* faith!

C H O O S E   T O   B E   F A I T H - FULL   T O D A Y.

DRIVING ON THE ROAD OF FAITH

Turn away from evil and do what is good;
seek peace and pursue it.
(PSALM 34:14)

Living by faith is a lot like driving a car.

The driver usually has a destination in mind. The destination for the person of faith is heaven!

The driver is wise to know the rules of the road. The rules of faith can be found in the Bible.

The driver needs to take good care of the car—maintaining the correct tire pressure and degree of tire tread, maintaining sufficient levels of oil and other necessary engine-related fluids, making sure the headlights, brakes, and taillights work properly, and so forth. The Christian must also seek to *maintain* a close relationship with the Lord—that is the key to maintaining faith.

A driver must maintain a safe speed—mindful of road conditions, weather conditions, and other drivers. The person of faith does the same in relationships with all whom he encounters—mindful of where *they* are in their faith walk, mindful of needs that warrant addressing in faith, and mindful of situations that are "under repair" that perhaps can use a dose of faith-filled encouragement.

A driver must concentrate on the task at hand—no texting, no phoning, no allowing for distractions from other passengers. The person of faith must also remain focused, saying "no" to the temptations that would pull his eyes off the goal of the high calling of Christ.

A driver is frequently asked to be patient in road-construction delays, or delays caused by accidents or debris on the roadway. So, too, patience is required in every person's faith journey. Delays can be a good time for singing praises to the Lord.

The person of faith can always count on having the Lord as a passenger—and even more appropriately, see himself as the passenger in the spiritual vehicle driven by the Lord!

Enjoy your faith journey today!

YOU ARE ONE DAY CLOSER TO HEAVEN
TODAY THAN YOU WERE YESTERDAY!

PROFILE OF THE FAITHFUL

*You are showing faithfulness by whatever you do for
the brothers. . . . They have testified of your love.*

(3 JOHN 5–6)

How do you describe a person who has faith?

Here is a description of a faithful person given by Evelyn Underhill in her classic book, *The Fruit of the Spirit*:

"It means keeping everything in your charge in good order for love's sake, rubbing up the silver, polishing the glass even though you know the Master will not be looking 'round the pantry next weekend. . . . You have got to be the sort of cat who can be left alone with the canary, the sort of dog who follows, hungry and thirsty but tail up, to the very end of the day.

"Faithfulness is the quality of the friend, refusing no test and no trouble, loyal, persevering, not at the mercy of emotional ups and downs or getting tired when things are tiresome."

How do you know if you have this kind of faith?

George MacDonald offered this method: "Ask yourself whether you have this day done one thing because He said, 'Do it,' or once abstained because He said, 'Do not do it.' It is simply absurd to say you believe, or even want to believe, in Him, if you do not do anything He tells you."

How do you hear from God the way He desires for you to display your faith?

Ask Him to speak to you a "yes" or "no" response in every circumstance of your day. Also, open your eyes to *what* and *who* the Lord brings across your path. His desire is for you to speak the truth of God's Word to all whom you encounter, to help all whom you can, to give of your time, talent, and treasure in a way that produces good, and to refrain from evil.

SEEK TO DEVELOP THE REPUTATION

OF A "PERSON OF FAITH"!

WHICH WAY?

[The prophet Elijah said,] "How long will you hesitate between two opinions? If Yahweh is God, follow Him. But if Baal, follow him." But the people didn't answer him a word.

(1 KINGS 18:21)

Years ago, a major evangelistic campaign swept America with the slogan "One Way!" A Christian pundit recently suggested that America needs a new slogan: "*This* Way!"

In the book of Philippians, the apostle Paul presents two diametrically opposed approaches to life. Furthermore, Paul regards every Christian as *choosing* with their will to pursue one path or the other—both cannot be pursued simultaneously.

The apostle Paul wrote about the following:

- Two destinations—either heaven, a destination that involves resurrection from death and transformation into a person with a glorious body like Christ's, or a destination of total destruction. Those who do not *believe* in heaven will feel little reason for spiritual discipline or for sharing the gospel message.
- Two lifestyles—either the pursuit of godly values and behaviors, which will inevitably provoke a degree of suffering and persecution by the ungodly, or a pursuit of sensual pleasures and

lusts. Those who do not believe lifestyle matters will do whatever "feels good" to them.

- Two great forces or powers—the power of the Holy Spirit working in us and through us, or the power of our own personal self-centered ambitions. Those who do not want to submit to God will not care what God says.

Our choices about what *we will believe and what we will do with our faith* ultimately make us either a friend of Christ or an "enemy of the cross." Those who *believe* in heaven, and the importance of living in a godly way according to the Bible's commandments, and who want the power of the Holy Spirit at work in them, are going to *become* people of faith who engage in activities that exalt Christ.

Examine what you truly *believe*. You will likely gain new insight into why you are making the daily, practical choices you are making.

CHOOSE TO LIVE A LIFE THAT IS INFORMED
AND DIRECTED BY YOUR FAITH IN GOD.

CHARGE!

[Paul wrote to Timothy,] "I remind you to keep
ablaze the gift of God that is in you."
(2 TIMOTHY 1:6)

*L*et us go forth to love and serve the Lord!" the pastor proclaimed as the final words of the Sunday morning worship service. All in the congregation responded, "Thanks be to God!"

Mom smiled as her thirteen-year-old son Chip then softly "sung" a brief little musical phrase and added the word "Charge!" as they turned to leave their pew and exit the church.

Mom recognized Chip's "comment" as something he likely had said with other fans at the previous Friday night high-school football game. She smiled again at the remembrance that she, too, had encouraged *her* football team at dozens of games to "Charge!" forward, annihilate the opposing team, and score a big win.

Later that day, she said to Chip, "I liked what you had to say at the end of the church service this morning . . . you know, *dum toda dum, dum dum*—CHARGE!"

"Yeah," Chip responded, "It made me want to go out and kick the devil to the curb."

"I've been thinking this afternoon that we ought to come up with some *faith* cheers for our family—things that we could say to ourselves as we leave the house each morning and go out to take on the day."

"Like what?" Chip said.

"Well, maybe like GO JESUS! WIN WIN WIN."

Chip grimaced. "Or maybe," he offered, "FIGHT FOR THE FAITH. FIGHT FIGHT FIGHT. Or, PUSH HIM BACK, PUSH HIM BACK, PUSH THE DEVIL W-A-Y BACK."

"That's the spirit," said Mom. "If there's a cheer worth cheering, it's got to be a cheer for God's will to prevail on this earth—and in our lives."

Chip grinned. "GIMME A *G*. GIMME AN *O*. GIMME A *D*. WHAT DOES IT SPELL?"

Mom chimed in, "GO, GOD, GO!"

DEVELOP YOUR OWN FAITH CHEER TODAY, AND THEN CHARGE INTO YOUR DAY WITH CONFIDENCE OF A WIN!

"GET OFF MY PORCH!"

The righteous cry out, and the LORD hears,
and delivers them from all their troubles.

(PSALM 34:17)

Eighty-year-old Harriet had gone to her front door after hearing unusual sounds coming from her front porch. She was mildly irritated at the interruption—she had been making a pie crust. She hurriedly opened the door, and to her surprise she saw, not the rummaging neighborhood dogs she expected to see, but rather, a large, unkempt man standing there. He held a knife in one hand and a screwdriver in the other. He obviously had forced open the screen door and was attempting to damage the lock on her front door to gain entrance into her house!

Harriet mustered her strength and stood as tall as she could stand—which was only five feet and one inch, and *commanded* the would-be intruder, "In the name of Jesus, you get off my porch and don't ever come back!"

When the police arrived later to get a description of the potential home invader, Harriet's first impulse was to say, "Well, he looked like the devil," but she swallowed that idea and gave as detailed a description as she could about his appearance and the direction he had gone when he left her property.

"Weren't you frightened?" one of the policeman asked.

"Not really," said Harriet. "That man was no match for God, and I knew God was with me."

"How did you know that?" the other policeman asked.

"It was obvious. He had sent three big angels to stand on my porch. This guy may have been able to squash me with his little finger, but he was no match for *them*!"

God's promise to you today as a believer in Christ Jesus is that if you will *resist* the devil, he *MUST flee from you.* You may not see the angels God sends to act on your behalf, but they are there nonetheless!

RESIST IN THE NAME OF JESUS ANY PERSON WHO SEEKS TO HARM GOD'S CHILD—YOU!

Rescue Assured

"Call on Me in a day of trouble;
I will rescue you, and you will honor Me."

(Psalm 50:15)

*I*magine you are in a row boat alone as you cross a lake, and suddenly, the boat springs a leak and water begins to fill your little craft—not quickly but insistently. As you look around at the shoreline before and behind you, you find nobody in sight, nobody to hear a cry for help!

Let us further suppose that you cannot swim well, and even if you could, the water is icy cold. You likely would be overcome by hypothermia before you could ever reach the shore. As you begin to cling to the water-logged sides of your little craft, you wonder if you might possibly be able to bail out the rising water with your hands. Fearing that this might not work, panic begins to set in. Hope begins to go down even as *you* go down into the water.

But now, let us assume that you remember you have your cell phone in a pocket that is still dry! You quickly reach for it, call on your speed dial the number for the lake's rescue patrol. Just as you are about to go under with the rowboat, you hear the sound of the rescue boat's outboard motor headed your way. You are saved!

The story is a good metaphor for the way life works for a person who does not have faith in Christ Jesus—and therefore has no genuine relationship with God. When life's carefully laid plans seem to "spring a leak" and difficulties take on the nature of a crisis, those without a "savior" have little hope. On the other hand, those who know Whom to call and who make the call with full assurance that God's help is on the way, know spiritually and practically what it means to experiencing Christ's "saving" power.

Trust Jesus today to be your SAVIOR
in all the ways you need saving!

WORDS OF FAITH

*If there is any moral excellence and if there is
any praise—dwell on these things.*

(PHILIPPIANS 4:8)

Those who first found the little journal were amazed at the words they read within it. Readers still are astonished:

"In the evening, when I lie in bed and end my prayers with the words, 'I thank You, God, for all that is good and dear and beautiful,' I am filled with joy. Then I think about 'the good' of going into hiding, of my health and with my whole being of the 'dearness' of Peter . . . and of the world, nature, beauty and all, all that is exquisite and fine.

"I don't think then of all the misery, but of the beauty that still remains. . . .

"I've found that there is always some beauty left—in nature, sunshine, freedom, in yourself, these can all help you. Look at these things, then you find yourself again, and God, and then you regain your balance. And whoever is happy will make others happy too. He who has courage and faith will never perish in misery!"

The words were those penned in a diary kept by Anne Frank, a victim of the Holocaust in World War II. She died in a concentration camp just months after writing this entry.

Faith offers a perspective on the totality of life—both specific experiences and a composite of all experience. It is a perspective that sees life as having as much or more *good* in it than evil. On the basis of what? On the basis that God is 100 percent good, *all the time.* God is present, *all the time.* And, God is in control of all things, *all the time.*

Such a perspective produces courage for the day, even though the greater "whole" of life may not be fully in focus.

KEEP YOUR FOCUS ON GOD'S GOODNESS!

FAITH FOR THE SMALL THINGS

*[Jesus said,] "If you believe, you will receive
whatever you ask for in prayer."*
(MATTHEW 21:22)

I don't think I can ever have *big* faith," a woman confessed to
a pastoral counselor. "I have enough trouble just believing in
God for the small things."

"How do you know they are small?" the pastor asked.

Most people think of big problems as those that have the power to
destroy their lives as they know them—the dreaded terminal medical
diagnosis, a lawsuit against their business, an impending divorce,
a child running away from home. Faith is *required* in times such
as these!

What do you see as "small" things that require faith? Is it an act
of your faith to get out of bed in the morning? To continue with a
desire to remain sober, or to continue a diet? What about sending a
child to another person's home for an overnight stay? Do you need
faith to walk from the bus stop to your apartment since you heard
the news of a neighborhood crime? In truth, these things may *be* life-
threatening issues.

Are there things that you rarely see as needing a faith application?
Do you take for granted that the company for whom you work will

continue to be able to provide you a paycheck? Do you assume that you will remain in good health? Do you assume that the appliances in your home will continue to work? Do you assume that your child will continue to be a "good kid" impervious to peer temptations? Aren't these areas worthy of *active* faith?

The wise conclusion is that we do not *know* which issues of life are little or big when it comes to a need for faith. *All* of life requires a faith response. Choose to say, "I believe in *You*, Lord," about *everything* you face in a day, about *every* relationship, *every* setback or opportunity.

ASSUME THAT ALL OF LIFE NEEDS
AN APPLICATION OF FAITH!

THANKS AND TRUST

*In everything, through prayer and petition with
thanksgiving, let your requests be made known to God.
And the peace of God, which surpasses every thought,
will guard your hearts and minds in Christ Jesus.*

(PHILIPPIANS 4:6–7)

"How is Kathleen doing?" Sarah asked Bob, Kathleen's husband. "We had a good day of thanking and trusting God," Bob replied.

"I'm not sure I know what you mean," Sarah said.

"Well, when an aide brought in breakfast to her hospital room, we said, 'Thank You, God. We're trusting You that Kathleen will be able to eat a few bites' . . . and she did."

"Later in the day, we said, 'Thank You, God. We're trusting You to give Kathleen the strength to stand up.' And . . . she stood up."

"Just a few minutes ago, we said, 'Thank You, God, for peaceful sleep. We're trusting You to let Kathleen fall asleep without added pain meds.' She just fell asleep."

"As long as we keep thanking God and trusting God, we have a good day," Bob concluded.

"This is an amazing way for everybody to live," the friend replied thoughtfully. "Thank and trust—I'm going to try it in my own life."

The next day she found herself saying, "Thank You, God, for a smooth drive to work. I'm trusting You for no delays on the freeway." She arrived at work ten minutes earlier than usual. "Thank You, God, for helping me with my work. I'm trusting You to help me finish the big project that is due tomorrow." She had the report printed by three in the afternoon. "Thank You, God, for a good parent-teacher conference at my child's school. I'm trusting You to lead me to ask the questions I need to ask." She had one of her best parent-teacher conferences ever.

What might you thank God for helping you do—in *advance*? What might you voice as a statement of trust to the Lord?

THANK AND TRUST!

HOME RUN FAITH

Be strengthened by the Lord and by His vast strength.

(EPHESIANS 6:10)

"I'm going to hit a home run today," Andy said with great confidence. "I can just feel it! I've asked God to help me hit a home run and I just know it is going to happen."

Dad smiled. "I sure hope that happens for you, son."

"Don't say it that way, Dad," Andy chided. "Say, 'Andy, you are going to do it!'"

Dad didn't respond other than to tousle Andy's hair and slap him affectionately on the back. "Go get 'em," he said.

Andy didn't hit a home run in that day's game. His first time at bat, he struck out. He nevertheless flashed a big smile at Dad in the stands. His second time at bat, he hit a single, and later crossed home plate when another player hit a triple. Andy flashed another smile as Dad cheered.

On his third trip to bat, Andy hit a double. On the fourth time at bat, he hit the game-winning triple.

Back in their car on the ride home, Andy said, "I didn't hit a home run but I sure was sneaking up on it!" he said. "If the game had just gone into extra innings, I *would* have hit a home run."

"Do you want to stop by and get a milkshake?" Dad asked.

"No," said Andy, "I'd rather stop by the batting cages. I've still got some hitting in me!"

What are you believing God to help you do today? An old saying proclaims, "If you aim for the moon and miss, you'll still land among the stars." The faith version of that may well be, "If you aim for the very best and trust God to help you, He'll help you do *your* very best and that will be sufficient in His eyes."

SWING FOR THE FENCES WITH YOUR FAITH TODAY.

Heaven Bound

*Now this is His command: that we believe in the name
of His Son Jesus Christ. . . . The one who keeps His
commands remains in Him, and He in him.*

(1 John 3:23–24)

Dorothy was facing a serious heart surgery, one that the doctors told her was very risky. She called for her pastor and said, "I need to know for *sure* that if I die on that operating table, I'm going to heaven."

"Do you believe God tells the truth in the Bible?" the pastor asked.

"Yes," Dorothy said. "God doesn't lie."

"And have you confessed your sins to God and asked Him to forgive you?"

"Yes."

"Do you believe that Jesus is the Son of God? Do you believe He is the Lord who died on the cross for your sins and rose from the dead?"

"Yes, yes, and yes."

"Well, listen to what the Bible says," the pastor said as he took a small Bible out of his coat pocket and opened it. He read, "'If we confess our sins, He is faithful and righteous to forgive us our sins and to cleanse us from all unrighteousness.' That's in 1 John 1:9. And now hear what Romans 10:9 says, 'If you confess with your mouth, "Jesus is

Lord," and believe in your heart that God raised Him from the dead, you will be saved.'"

The pastor turned to yet another part of his Bible. "And one more, Dorothy, one you know well. John 3:16, 'For God loved the world in this way: He gave His One and Only Son, so that everyone who believes in Him will not perish but have eternal life.'"

"Okay, Pastor," Dorothy said. "I'm ready! If I die tomorrow, I'm going to heaven. But you can still say a prayer that I don't die. I've got a lot more living I'd *like* to do here before I go *there*."

"Good perspective," the pastor said. "Live for then and hope for now!"

KNOWING YOUR ULTIMATE DESTINATION CAN
HELP YOU PLAN TODAY'S JOURNEY.

Preparing for the Test

*If you accept my words and store up my commands
within you . . . then you will understand the fear of
the Lord and discover the knowledge of God.*

(Proverbs 2:1, 5)

"Mom," Sissy said, "I need for you to pray *really* hard that I do well on my spelling test tomorrow."

"I'll pray," Mom said, "but let me ask you—have you *studied* for this test?"

Sissy hesitated. "I've looked at all the words twice," she finally said.

"Let me tell you what worked for me when I was your age. And yes, we had spelling tests back then, too!"

Mom continued, "You need to write out the words. I found that I needed to write out a word seven times before it really stuck in my mind."

"So I should go write out all the words seven times?" Sissy said.

"It's a good idea to try," Mom said, and then added, "Here's the deal I'll make with you. Go to your room and write out each of the words seven times. Turn off your music and really concentrate on what you are writing. And tomorrow, I'll pray seven times that you do well on your test!"

Sissy nodded and did as Mom asked.

Of course she scored 100 percent!

Educational researchers tell us that information that is repeated at least seven times has a very high likelihood of being recalled readily and accurately. This seems to hold true for people of all ages, and the effect seems to be especially potent if a person repeats or repeatedly learns information over a period of several days.

What a good reason to *memorize* faith-building verses from the Bible! Read a verse repeatedly until you can recite it perfectly without looking at the text and then recite it to yourself seven times over the next several days. Seal it into your heart and mind. Doing this just may help *you* to pass an important test in *your* life.

R EHEARSE FAITH'S ANSWERS BEFORE YOU NEED THEM.

Extreme Skateboarder

[Jesus said,] "All things
are possible with God."

*H*ow does he *do* that?" Linda asked as she watched her friend
Lisa's son Jim practice what she considered to be "extreme
skateboarding" tricks at a local skateboarding park.

Felicity, another friend at the park with Linda and Lisa, said, "*My*
question would be, how did he ever live long enough to *do* these tricks
without breaking his neck before now?"

Renee chimed in, "*My* question is, why did you ever let him get into
skateboarding in the first place?"

The three friends were all scared for Jim but were also in awe at his
athleticism and the difficulty of the tricks.

Lisa said, "I'll take those questions one at a time. First, I let Jimmy
skate on the flat driveway by our house and I made him wear a helmet
and knee and elbow pads. He began going to the skateboard park after
school without my really knowing about it. When I found out, I made
him work with an instructor who assured me he was very concerned
about Jimmy's safety.

"Second, Jimmy didn't start *out* doing these very difficult tricks.
He built up to them over time.

"And third, he had an attitude about each trick he tried: 'I *believe* I can do this.' His belief was based on previous success, and the teaching of his coach."

Renee smiled. "I think you've been asked these questions before. You have your answers down!"

Lisa replied, "You bet! I've had lots of practice *believing* God that Jimmy will not get hurt!"

Faith grows the more we use it, and the more we apply it to bigger and bigger needs in our lives.

We must prepare, practice, and never presume. In the end, faith declares, "To God be the glory! Great things *He* has done and is doing."

FAITH IS INTENDED TO GROW.

THE FOCUS OF FAITH

[Jesus said,] "Man must not live
on bread alone but on every word
that comes from the mouth of God."

(MATTHEW 4:4)

*B*ut . . . I had *faith* that I was going to win this match!" Mary said. "I'm a much better tennis player than Wendi."

"Was your faith focused on winning the match . . . or on God to give you what is best?" her mother asked, eager to console her daughter in the loss but also recognizing that Mary might also need to learn something about faith.

"What do you mean?" Mary asked.

"God wants us to trust *Him* with everything we do. He knows what is best for us. And sometimes His answer to us about something we want—even want a *lot*—is 'no,' 'later,' or a 'something better,'" Mom said.

"But why wouldn't it be God's desire for me to win this tennis match?" Mary said.

"I don't know," Mom replied. "Why not ask Him, 'What is it You are trying to teach me in this?'" Mary nodded in agreement. "I will," she said. "Maybe there's something God wants me to do to make me an even better player."

Not knowing about this conversation, the next day Mary's tennis coach came to her and said, "I think we need to work on changing your serve." Mary had thought she had a strong serve, and the change her coach was asking her to make was difficult. After a couple of weeks, however, of practicing the new technique, Mary started to see a benefit. Her serve became much faster and more accurate. By the time the season was over, Mary had moved into the number two position on her team. The next year, she was number one and had a strong reputation for the best serve in the league. A local college offered her a full scholarship for tennis!

What is the focus of *your* faith?

PUT YOUR TRUST IN THE ONE WHO HAS JUST
THE RIGHT ANSWERS FOR YOUR BEST.

A WAY THROUGH THE MAZE

This is what the LORD of Hosts says: If you walk in
My ways and keep My instructions, you will both
rule My house and take care of My courts.

(ZECHARIAH 3:7)

*D*id you have a good time?" Mom eagerly asked as Scotti climbed into the back seat behind her.

"Not really," the eleven-year-old replied.

"But it's the *amusement* park," Mom replied with an upbeat attitude. "You are supposed to be *amused*. And it has a *fun* house! It's supposed to be *fun*."

"Well, it wasn't that much fun to me!" Scotti said.

"Why not?" Mom asked.

"That *fun* house was a maze," Scotti said. "A stupid maze! And it was filled with mirrors that made you look tall and thin, or short and fat, and everywhere you turned, you just saw a gross reflection, and there was no way out." Tears began to flow as Scotti admitted, "It was scary, Mom. I started to panic. I wasn't sure I would *ever* find my way out."

Mom pulled the car to the side of the road to give Scotti her full attention. "But you're all right now, sweetie," she said, reaching back to put her hand on Scotti's knee. "And you don't ever have to go back there if you don't want. But tell me, what did you do? How did you find your way out?"

"I started to pray—'God help me get out of here. I promise I'll never go into a place like this again,'" Scotti said. "And God showed me that if I looked down at the floor I would see which part of the floor had the most scuff marks—and this would be the path through the maze."

"Brilliant!" Mom said. "Sometimes when we cry out to God, He shows us something we hadn't seen before—and that *is* the way to go."

After you pray in faith, look around. Is there something you *now* see that you didn't see before?

G<small>OD HAS A WAY THROUGH LIFE'S MAZE</small>!

PRAYER FOR FAITH

[Jesus said,] "Let the little children come to Me. Don't stop
them, for the kingdom of God belong to such as these."
(MARK 10:14)

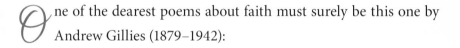

One of the dearest poems about faith must surely be this one by
Andrew Gillies (1879–1942):

Last night my little boy confessed to me
Some childish wrong;
And kneeling at my knee,
He prayed with tears—
"Dear God, make me a man
Like Daddy—wise and strong.
I know You can."
Then while he slept
I knelt beside his bed,
Confessed my sins,
And prayed with low-bowed head,
"O God, make me a child
Like my child here—
Pure, guileless,
Trusting Thee with faith sincere."

God's Word admonishes us to have faith as a little child—to come before God with a trust born of total dependency. Jesus told His disciples, "Let the little children come to Me. Don't stop them, for the kingdom of God belongs to such as these" (Mark 10:14).

The good news is that the Lord promises us that if we will trust Him and allow Him to do His work in us, He will transform us into a spiritually mature person, reflecting the nature of Christ Jesus in the world. God's Word to us in Romans 8:29 is that we will "be conformed to the image of His Son."

PRAY WITH FAITH TO BE MORE LIKE CHRIST.
AFTER THAT IS A PRAYER GOD ALWAYS
ANSWERS WITH A YES!

A BETTER BLESSING

The LORD will fulfill His purpose for me.

(PSALM 138:8)

Joan had her heart set on becoming a foreign-exchange student. One particular program that sent high-school students abroad for eight weeks during the summer months caught her attention. She quickly completed the application form and entered the competition. Those who knew Joan well told her repeatedly they thought she was the sure winner. For her part, Joan felt very good about the competition's interview and was already starting to anticipate *where* she might be assigned. She was hoping for someplace in England, Scotland, or Ireland!

Then came word that Joan had *not* won the competition. She had not even been named the runner-up.

Her father could tell how deeply disappointed she was, and he suggested, "Let's pray about this and trust that God has something even *better* for you down the line. Perhaps it will be something better for this summer, or some better way to travel and study overseas."

Joan agreed, although a bit reluctantly. "I can't imagine what it will be, but I'll pray with you."

"Faith isn't based on our imagination," Dad said gently. "It's about trusting God for His best blessings."

That summer, Joan worked with children in a tutoring program to help them learn English. Most of the students were Hispanic, and over the summer Joan discovered that not only did her "students" learn English, but she learned Spanish! Joan enjoyed her newly acquired language so much—in part because it had seemed so easy for her to pick up—that she majored in Spanish when she went to college. And during her junior year, she won an all-expenses-paid award for spending an entire semester in Barcelona, Spain.

"And guess what?" she told her dad. "I get to spend two weeks in the British Isles at the end of the semester!"

GOD'S BEST IS ALWAYS BETTER THAN
ANYTHING WE CAN IMAGINE.

No Substitute for Deciding

Shadrach, Meshach, and Abednego replied to the king...
"If the God we serve exists, then He can rescue us from
the furnace of blazing fire, and He can rescue us from
the power of you, the king. But even if He does not rescue
us, we want you as king to know that we will not serve
your gods or worship the gold statue you set up."
(DANIEL 3:16–18)

A story that former president Ronald Reagan enjoyed telling had to do with an experience he had in his childhood.

According to the story, Reagan's aunt took him to a cobbler one day to have a pair of shoes custom-made for him. The shoemaker asked, "Do you want a square toe or a round one?" Reagan hemmed and hawed, apparently weighing the benefits of each style, and finally the shoemaker said, "Come back in a day or two and tell me what you want."

Several days later the cobbler saw Reagan on the street and asked him what he had decided. "I haven't made up my mind," he answered.

The shoemaker replied, "Very well, your shoes will be ready tomorrow." When Reagan picked up the shoes he discovered that one had a round toe, the other a square toe!

Reagan said in telling his story, "Looking at those shoes every day taught me a lesson. If you don't make your own decisions, somebody else will make them for you."

Having faith does not mean that we leave all *decision making* to God. Rather, it means that we trust God to *reveal* to us the decisions that He desires for us to make! Some of His revealing comes to us as we read the Bible, some as He leads us to recall the consequences of past decisions, and some as we listen to the wise counsel of other Christians.

God has a plan and a "best choice"—it is our responsibility to discern it and to act decisively. If we err in our decision making, we can always trust God to correct us. On the other hand, if we fail to decide, the devil is likely to insert his opinion and prompt others to make *very bad decisions* for us.

TRUST GOD TODAY TO HELP YOU
MAKE THE GODLY DECISIONS.

DAY-BY-DAY FAITH

By faith Noah, after he was warned about what was not yet seen and motivated by godly fear, built an ark to deliver his family.

(HEBREWS 11:7)

Boy, some of those Bible people had really big faith," Johnny said on the family's way home from church and Sunday school.

"Anybody particular in mind?" Dad asked.

"Our story in Sunday school today was about Noah. He sure had big faith to build a boat like the ark that would survive the big flood."

"Yes," said Dad. "Noah had faith in God, but I don't think he knew he was building a boat."

"But that's what the ark was," Johnny said.

"Noah heard God tell him to build a very big, watertight building—it was like a big box," Dad said. "I don't think Noah ever dreamed that building would float. He only knew it was a boat *after* the flood. Noah had faith that God had spoken. He had faith to start building and start gathering animals."

"Our teacher said it took him hundreds of years to build the ark," Johnny said.

"Yes, and I think that Noah got up every day and had faith to do just what God showed him to do *on that day*. One day that might have been mixing up tar. On another day it might have been faith to find two zebras. And one day God told him to load the box and shut the door. That was a special day for faith!"

"And then when it started to rain, he had to have faith that the ark would stay watertight," said Johnny. "And then one day he had faith he could get out of the ark," said Johnny.

"Right!" said Dad. "Every day was a new day for the faith he needed . . . for that day."

"Well, I can tell you this," Johnny's sister Gail piped up. "*Mrs.* Noah had big faith!"

TRUST GOD TO GIVE YOU THE FAITH

YOU NEED FOR TODAY.

FAITHALISTIC

If you do not stand firm in your faith,
then you will not stand at all.

(ISAIAH 7:9)

Que sera, sera," Dee said.

"Why are you saying that?" her older sister Kendra asked.

"Well, it means 'what will be, will be,'" Dee said.

"I know what the Spanish means," Kendra said. "But you sound so fatalistic. You're dealing with your future. *You* have something to say about the direction it is going. You have goals and dreams that are worth voicing."

"Maybe," said Dee. "Or maybe it is better to go with the flow and let things unfold whatever way they are going to unfold."

"Have you talked to God about this?" Kendra asked.

"No," said Dee.

"You mean, you're walking blindly into the future?" Kendra asked, becoming increasingly concerned.

"Yes, more or less," Dee said. "Actually, I think I'm letting my future 'happen' without any interference. I'm getting into the flow, believing that the river knows where it's going."

"That's mumbo-jumbo," Kendra countered. "It certainly isn't faith. If you haven't *asked* God to guide your actions, and if you aren't *trusting* God to lead you step by step toward *His* outcome, it isn't faith. From my perspective, you are giving up and letting other people and perhaps even the forces of evil direct your life. You are being so passive that you are likely to arrive at a destination you won't want when you get there. You *are* being fatalistic."

"So what do you suggest I do?" Dee asked.

"Get on your knees and ask God to show you *His* plan—what you are to say and do, and when. Trust God with this. And then, get up and have the courage to walk out what He reveals to you. Be *faithalistic*, Dee, not fatalistic!"

BE FAITHALISTIC, NOT FATALISTIC,

ABOUT THE DAY AHEAD OF YOU.

In Alignment

*Obey Me, and then I will be your God, and you
will be My people. You must follow every way
I command you so that it may go well with you.*
(Jeremiah 7:23)

*E*verybody in town knew Mr. Paul. He had been the high school
auto mechanics and driver's ed teacher for decades.

Since his retirement, Mr. Paul had offered free auto maintenance
lessons to students in his own well-equipped garage behind his home.
Female students came on Saturday mornings, male students on
Saturday afternoons.

Mr. Paul was also known as a man of spiritual wisdom—he had
taught Sunday school classes at his church for thirty years. It was
natural for him to infuse biblical stories and Christian principles into
his auto-maintenance lessons.

"Your faith needs to be in *alignment*," Mr. Paul said on one particular
Saturday. "Just like the tires of this car need to be in alignment so they
wear evenly and avoid a blowout, so your faith 'tire' needs to be in
alignment with other parts of your life so you don't get stressed out."

"What other parts?" one student asked.

"Faith needs to be lined up with the Bible. God doesn't want you
believing for things that aren't yours to have according to the Good

Book. Two, faith needs to line up with the way God has hard-wired you as a person. You have to know the gifts God has given to you and work on them *with* God. And third, you need to use your faith to prepare you for the destination that God has for you. Not everybody is supposed to do the same thing, or in the same place. If faith is in alignment with the Bible, God's gifts, and God's goals, you'll have a much smoother ride in life.

"It's all about the ride," Mr. Paul concluded. "Do things His way and keep your life in order."

He added with a chuckle, "And *then,* work with others to fix the roads . . . *please!*"

KEEP YOUR FAITH IN ALIGNMENT!

GOD'S INVITATION

The LORD will establish you as His holy people, as He swore to you, if you obey the commands of the LORD your God and walk in His ways.
(DEUTERONOMY 28:9)

Come on, Josh," Grandma said, "God is inviting us to work with Him in the garden."

Josh loved his grandmother, but he wasn't all that excited about working in her very large garden, which had a small vineyard at one end and a few fruit trees at the other end. He would rather spend his afternoon playing video games inside.

"Grams," he said, "I don't think God *needs* our help. We need His help but He doesn't really need *our* help, does He?"

"Here in the garden or in life as a whole?" Grandma asked.

"Both," Josh said.

Grandma nodded. She set down her basket of ripe vegetables and reached up to pick fruit from a nearby tree.

"You have a point," she said. Josh seized on her agreement to add, "God can do *anything*, Grams. He grows stuff all around the world. He can grow a garden without your doing so much work in it all the time."

"Yes," Grandma agreed. "God can certainly *do* anything He desires. He could make a basket of ripe fruit appear on the front stoop every day. But that really isn't the point. God *invites* us to work *with Him*. He invites us to plant and water and hoe. He invites us to pick fruit when it's ripe so it doesn't fall and rot on the ground."

"Do you know why God *invites* us to work *with Him*?" Grandma asked.

Josh admitted, "Not really."

"So we can enjoy being outdoors and being productive. Also, so we can have fresh peach cobbler for dessert tonight and feel thankful for it. The process is all about good rewards for *us*. God does the growing . . ."

". . . but we get to do the eating!" Josh said, suddenly eager to help pick peaches.

ACCEPT GOD'S INVITATION TO

WORK WITH HIM TODAY.

A Spiritual Knowing

*Love the LORD your God, obey Him, and remain
faithful to Him. For He is your life.*
(DEUTERONOMY 30:20)

*J*ill's brother Gregory was being prepped for open heart surgery
when the lead surgeon stepped into the hallway, seemingly
intent on underscoring to Jill just how serious the operation would
be. "He will be in surgery all day," he said to her. "There is a fifty-fifty
chance that your brother will not live through this. He knows those
odds and seems to have accepted the fact that he may not survive the
operation. Your pastor is with him now."

Jill replied, "My brother is going to live."

"I just told you," the surgeon replied kindly but firmly, "that he
may not."

"I am not in denial," Jill said. "I know you are telling me what you
think I need to know, based on the facts of my brother's condition. I
also know that you, as a surgical team, are facing some things that
you have never faced in a heart surgery before." The surgeon nodded
in agreement.

"And here's what I am saying to you, sir," Jill said politely but also
firmly. "I am going to be praying for you and your entire team all
day, for wisdom and skill and insights beyond anything you've ever

experienced in an operating room. I am praying for a *speedy* recovery for my brother. My brother is going to live! I *know* it"

"How do you *know* that?" the surgeon asked, in a voice barely above a whisper. He was skeptical but had a degree of respect for her optimism.

"I don't know it with my mind, sir," Jill replied. "I know it with my faith. I know it in my spirit. You do your best. I'll do my best praying and believing. We will talk at the end of the day."

Gregory was back at work five weeks later.

LISTEN TO WHAT GOD SPEAKS TO YOUR SPIRIT.

FAITH FOR DYING

The LORD is near the brokenhearted;
He saves those crushed in spirit.

(PSALM 34:18)

I think it could be tonight," Dad said to his two adult children as they stood outside the hospital near midnight.

"I agree," Bonnie said. "I told Mom good-bye tonight as I held her hand and prayed."

Bud nodded that he had done the same.

Mom had been in a coma for several days, growing weaker and weaker, her breathing more shallow, her skin more translucent. The family had known that Mom had been dying more than living for several weeks. Their great love for her had kept them believing for a last-minute miracle in her battle with cancer. They were intensely sad, but not in shock.

"I didn't know that it takes so much faith for dying," Bud said softly.

"I know what you mean," Bonnie said as she took his hand. "I've been struggling to believe that this is Mom's time to go live in the Lord's near presence. I've been believing that her end will be just what the prayer service says: 'holy, good, and peaceful.' I've been believing that we are going to be okay and that God is going to help each of us get through these next few days."

"And weeks and months," Dad added. "I've been asking God to confirm all my beliefs about heaven and how perfect it is and how much joy Mom will have there."

"I asked Mom about a month ago if she feared dying," Bonnie said. "She told me she had more faith for dying than for dealing with her pain and immobility. She said, 'I believe Jesus will be waiting for me.' I believe what Mom believes."

To that, Bud said a soft "amen." And Dad added, "There *is* a faith required for dying. And faith for continuing to live. May God strengthen both."

LIVE FULLY IN FAITH SO YOU MIGHT

DIE PEACEFULLY IN FAITH.

A Working Definition

*Without faith it is impossible to please God, for the
one who draws near to Him must believe that He
exists and rewards those who seek Him.*

(HEBREWS 11:6)

*D*o you have a "working definition" for faith?

The most basic definition, of course, is that faith is *believing*, and in a spiritual context, faith is *believing God*.

Christians are called upon to believe that God *exists*. They are called upon to believe that God is a *Rewarder*—that He bestows the blessings of His presence, provision, and protection upon those who love and serve Him. Through the ages Christians have been called upon to acknowledge God as omnipresent (both eternal and in every moment), omniscient (all-knowing, all-wise), and omnipotent (all-powerful in His ability to both create and sustain).

But how does faith manifest itself in day-to-day living? How does faith function? Here is the way one poet, V. Raymond Edman, phrased his working definition:

FAITH is dead to doubts—
Dumb to discouragement,
Blind to impossibilities,

Knows nothing but success.

FAITH lifts its hand up through

The threatening clouds,

Lays hold of Him who has

all power in heaven and on earth.

FAITH makes the uplook good,

The outlook bright,

The inlook favorable.

And the future glorious.

WHAT IS YOUR WORKING DEFINITION

FOR FAITH——IN YOUR LIFE?

A FAITH PACT

[Jesus said,] "If two of you on earth agree
about any matter that you pray for, it will be
done for you by My Father in heaven."

The story is told of an orphan girl in India who was desperate for a home. One day she approached a visiting missionary teacher from a nearby village and asked for help. The teacher replied that she had no room in her house at the present time, and no money to secure lodging. "But I will pray and ask God for His help," she said, "and you do the same." They entered into a faith pact, the two of them agreeing that the girl would have a home. As she began the walk back to her village, the teacher specifically asked God in her private prayers to make a way for *her* to give shelter to the girl in her home.

When the teacher returned home the next day, she found a letter from a friend in America. Enclosed was a small amount of money— just enough, in the teacher's opinion, to *start* providing for the orphan girl. She accepted the letter as God's answer, and the next morning, she called for a trusted associate to go to the neighboring village—a day's walk away—find the girl, and bring her back. She described the girl in detail and told him where to look.

To the teacher's surprise, the messenger returned with the girl in half the time she had anticipated. "How did you travel so quickly?" the teacher asked.

The messenger replied that he had found the girl halfway to the teacher's house as he walked the road between their villages. The girl spoke, "We both prayed to God for help. I had faith that God would help me and also faith that God would help you to help me. So I thought I might as well start walking."

AGREE WITH A CHRISTIAN FRIEND
IN FAITH FOR GOD'S ANSWER.

"I'll Do the Believing"

[Jesus said,] "Let it be done for you according to your faith!"
(MATTHEW 9:29)

Nearly sixty years ago, a mother brought her crippled son to an evangelistic rally, believing this would be a good time for her son to accept Jesus as His personal Savior, and also a good time for him to receive prayer. The preacher who was conducting the rally had a strong reputation for preaching a "salvation sermon," and also for praying for sick people.

As she had hoped, her son eagerly accepted Jesus Christ into his life and eagerly went forward for prayer.

The mother explained that her son had a degenerative disease, which had eaten away most of a major bone in his body. There was no known medical cure.

The evangelist shook his head. He had heard about the disease and its crippling effects. He said with sadness, "Ma'am, I have to be honest with you before God. I don't have faith to believe for your son to be healed."

The mother's eyes flashed as she said, "Sir, I'm not asking you to have faith. I'm asking you to pray your best prayer. You do the praying. *I'll* do the believing."

At that, he prayed fervently for the boy and then sighed with even greater sadness as the boy limped away.

Six months later, he saw this mother and son in a nearby city, but he hardly recognized them. The mother said, "We didn't come for prayer tonight. We came to tell you what happened. My son went back and had a second set of X-rays, and then at the doctors' insistence, a third set of X-rays. Bone has grown where there was no bone. My son's pain is gone. His limp is gone. He's going to live well and strong."

"Ma'am," the evangelist said, "it is *your* faith that God heard louder than he heard my prayer."

Faith speaks volumes.

WHAT GOD REQUIRES

The one who believes in the Son has eternal life.

(JOHN 3:36)

A pastor shared with his congregation one morning that he had experienced a "night vision" or a "spiritual dream" the previous night. He said, "I had arrived in heaven and was told to take a seat at a table, and to use the pen and paper provided there to write my earthly resume.

"I wrote out all my accomplishments and memberships, stating things as accurately and positively as I could. And then, I went to stand in line to present my 'report.'

"The angel read through my list. Finally, he asked, 'Is this what the Lord *asked* you to do?'

"I hung my head. I had to admit that some of the things on the list were things I had *wanted* to do, but which the Lord had never asked me to do. Some were things that other people had prompted or pressured me to do. A few things I believed to be commandments from the Bible that I, and all other Christians, were to do. But I had to admit to the angel, 'No, most of these things were not things the Lord directly and specifically asked me to do.'

"I was feeling very discouraged and then the angel smiled and said, 'Here in heaven you will do only what the Lord asks you to do, and you will find that to be a truly joyful way to live."

The pastor concluded, "I awoke from my dream with a firm resolution that from this day forward, I am going to do only what I *know* the Lord is commanding me to do. I am redirecting my faith to knowing and doing *only* God's plan for me—not the plans of men, not the plans I make for myself. I invite you to do the same."

DO WHAT GOD REQUIRES.

THE RELUCTANT PREACHER

[Jesus said,] "Just as Moses lifted up the snake in the wilderness, so the Son of Man must be lifted up, so that everyone who believes in Him will have eternal life."

(JOHN 3:14–15)

ohn Eggden had never preached a sermon, didn't want to, and had never needed to. He was, however, qualified to do so in his role as the deacon of his church in Colchester, England.

One Sunday morning in January of 1850, Eggden awoke to find his town buried in snow. His first thought was to stay home from church, but then he reconsidered. If he didn't go as the deacon, who would? So he put on his boots, gloves, hat, and coat and walked the six miles to the church.

Only thirteen other people joined Eggden that day—twelve members and one visitor, a thirteen-year-old boy. Even the pastor had stayed home and a couple of those present suggested they pray and adjourn. Eggden would hear none of that—he embarked on a full service, including a sermon that fell to him to preach.

Eggden mustered his faith and mounted the pulpit to preach a message that lasted only about ten minutes. He tried to make several points but wandered about in his sermonizing to the degree that he wasn't sure he made even one point. Toward the end of the sermon, however, he felt an uncharacteristic boldness come upon him. He lifted his eyes and looked straight at the boy and said, "Young man, look to Jesus. Look! Look! Look!"

The boy reported later, "I did look, and then and there the cloud on my heart lifted, the darkness rolled away, and at that moment I saw the sun."

The boy's name was Charles Haddon Spurgeon. He became known as England's "prince of preachers," whose sermons and writings are still circulated worldwide.

Have faith to say what God compels you to say today! A life just may be changed forever.

LOOK TO JESUS AND ENCOURAGE ALL
AROUND YOU TO DO THE SAME!

A New Understanding

*[Jesus said,] "For God loved the world
in this way: He gave His One and Only Son,
so that everyone who believes in Him
will not perish but have eternal life."*

(John 3:16)

One thing a believer in Christ can count on is that the Lord will work to "correct" any belief or behavior that is contrary to His desire for the believer. We do not need to know everything about anything before we act in faith. If we make a mistake in either what we believe or how we execute our faith, He'll show us our error and nudge us into the right way we should go, much the way a loving parent guides the errant curiosity of a wandering toddler.

Noted author Catherine Marshall wrote this about her misconceptions regarding faith:

"Much of my own problem with faith arose from an early misunderstanding of what faith is. First of all, I used to believe that faith had something to do with feeling. For example, when I had messed up some situation and had asked for forgiveness, then I would peer inside myself to see if I felt forgiven. If I could locate such feelings, then I was sure that God had heard and had forgiven me. Now I know that this is an altogether false test of faith.

"Another misconception I once had was that faith is trying to believe something one is fairly certain is not true. But faith is not hocus-pocus, opposed to knowledge and reality. In fact, faith does not go against experience at all; rather it appeals to experience.

"Perhaps one reason that the real meaning of faith eluded me personally for so many years was that it is so surprisingly simple, so practical. Faith in God is simply trusting Him enough to step out on that trust."

We each must be open to God's corrective guidance about faith.

ASK GOD TO TEACH YOU MORE TODAY ABOUT
THE POWER AND PURPOSE OF YOUR FAITH.

PUT TO THE TEST

"I will refine them as silver is refined
and test them as gold is tested.
They will call on My name,
and I will answer them.
I will say: They are My people,
and they will say: Yahweh is our God."

(ZECHARIAH 13:9)

Years ago a missionary in Brazil found himself deeply troubled by the local government policies that did little to promote economic stability or a better life for the rural citizens. The farmers who were part of his missionary church were routinely robbed of their land and their harvests, and sometimes their lives. The missionary was unwilling and unable to sit idly by, but rather than encourage direct protesting or a violent response from those who attended the church, he wrote repeatedly to US magazines and government officials about the plight of the people he served, asking for them to put pressure on the officials to change their ways.

Word of his letters and articles reached the local authorities, as might be expected, and for four days, the missionary was imprisoned and physically tortured by those who sought to "warn him" to stop all of his writing efforts.

The missionary stated that his only comfort during his imprison-ment was his faith. He recited Psalm 23 to himself almost nonstop for four days. Then, one of his torturers told him with a sneer that his friends at the church were praying for him. He felt elated and encouraged—not discouraged as his captors had thought. He felt strength surge through him.

After his release was secured through the intervention of American embassy officials, the missionary told his congregation and others back in America that he was grateful for his imprisonment and torture for this one reason: "I discovered with profound conviction that all the things I had been saying I believed for the past twenty years were *true*. I *really* believed."

Suffering had not diminished his faith, but strengthened it. That's what happens when genuine faith is put to a test. It is refined, becomes more real, and is strengthened.

SEE YOUR STRUGGLES AS AN OPPORTUNITY
FOR YOUR FAITH TO BE REFINED.

FIFTEEN QUESTIONS

*Test yourselves to see if you are
in the faith. Examine yourselves.*

(2 CORINTHIANS 13:5)

*T*wenty Questions is a popular game that has been played by many through the years. The game is also a good tool for getting acquainted with strangers, for deepening relationships, and for self-introspection. But what about faith—what about getting to know more about the Lord and deepening one's personal relationship with God?

Below are fifteen questions that are directly related to faith. Ponder them today. If your answer is "yes" to a question—what more might you contemplate or decide? If your answer is "no," explore the reason and potential consequences.

Then, find opportunity to talk about these questions with a family member, friend, or colleague. And pray about them, asking the Lord to reveal to you *His* truth that will give a stronger foundation to your *believing*. Add more questions that may come to mind!

1. Do you believe God exists?
2. Do you believe God is always good?
3. Do you believe God loves you?

4. Do you believe you have faith?

5. Do you believe God is a rewarder of those who diligently seek Him?

6. Do you believe a person can have a personal relationship with God?

7. Do you believe it is vital for you to apply faith to real needs and problems?

8. Do you routinely find ways to use your faith?

9. Do you believe faith can grow or become stronger?

10. Do you know what causes your faith to waver?

11. Do you know how to renew your faith?

12. Do you know how to share your faith in Christ with others?

13. Do you believe there is ever a time when faith is not required?

14. Do you see yourself as a person who trusts God daily?

15. Do you have an understanding about how acts of faith create a life of trust?

TRUST GOD TO HELP YOU ANSWER
YOUR HONEST QUESTIONS.

MUSTARD SEED

[Jesus said,] "If you have faith the size
of a mustard seed, you will tell this mountain,
'Move from here to there,' and it will move.
Nothing will be impossible for you."

(MATTHEW 17:20)

*M*ustard seeds are small, but the seeds of the mustard plants that grow in Israel are *especially* small! Each grain of seed is about the size of a grain of cayenne pepper—about the size of the period at the end of this sentence.

Mustard grows wild and prolific in the Middle East. The seeds are not used as a spice. For many, mustard plants are considered a weed, a nuisance. Mustard often grows along the banks of streams and lakes, where its roots cling to the soil, drawing moisture from the water source and helping the plant to grow to a height of twelve feet or taller. The weight of the tree often causes a collapse of the soil in which it grows, resulting in erosion of the river or lake side bank as tree and earth tumble into the waters.

Jesus used mustard as a metaphor to point out a critical truth about faith. If even the tiniest amount of faith is planted in the "soil" of a need or problem, it can take root and grow to the point that it can cause that need or problem to collapse and be swept away. Even a mountain of need cannot withstand the growing power of faith planted into it!

People sometimes say, "But I don't have *any* faith to plant." The Bible says otherwise (see Romans 12:3). It affirms that *every* person has been given a measure of faith—every person has at least some ability to *believe*. The truth revealed by Jesus is that if a person has at least *some* faith, that faith is going to be at *least* the size of one of the smallest seeds known on earth, a grain of mustard! Ask God to show you how and where to plant the faith you have.

PLANT YOUR FAITH AGAINST YOUR NEED!

What God Can Do

[Jesus said,] "Everything is possible to the one who believes."
(MARK 9:23)

*A*unt Lou," Jamie said during a spring-break visit to her home, "you seem to have faith for *everything*. You pray all the time and ask God to do stuff that sometimes seems impossible. I don't know anybody else who prays like you do."

"Do you see that God responds to faith?" Aunt Lou asked.

"Yeah, sometimes," Jamie said. "But there are lots of things that still are wrong—not just in the world, but in the lives of people we both know. Some of the other students at college have lots of really big problems that God doesn't seem to solve, even when I and others pray about them."

"That's true," said Aunt Lou, "which is all the more reason to pray. But I don't think we can ever conclude that God doesn't care, or that God isn't at work. We just may not see what God is doing behind the scenes of their lives."

"Do you think faith can work in every situation?" Jamie asked.

"Two things, Jamie," Aunt Lou said thoughtfully. "First, when I read the Bible I find lots of evidence that God wants us to pray and to have faith, and that He responds to those who have faith. Jesus said on a number of occasions to people He healed or delivered, 'Your faith has made you whole.' So, I want to be one of those who is praying and believing.

"Second, I know what I cannot do as a human being. But I do not know of anything *God* can't do. In fact, I'm eager to see what God might do next!"

"I'm all for *that*!" Jamie said. "I'm especially eager to see how God is going to answer our prayers for helping me pay next semester's tuition!"

RATHER THAN FOCUS ON WHAT YOU CANNOT
DO, FOCUS ON WHAT GOD CAN DO.

CLAIMING WHAT IS IMPORTANT

Remember the great and awe-inspiring Lord.

(NEHEMIAH 4:14)

*J*enny Lind was called "the Swedish Nightingale." Her operatic high soprano voice was acclaimed internationally, and she became one of the most successful and wealthiest artists of her time. Her many fans were shocked when she left the stage at a time when her singing was considered to be at its peak—few could understand how she could walk away from a career at its height.

Some speculated that she was secretly ill. Others wondered if she was experiencing mental depression. Still others thought she might be suffering from a broken heart. And for years, people expected her to make a "comeback," which never happened. Virtually nobody could understand how she could walk away so completely from such applause, fame, and money.

Jenny Lind, however, seemed content to pursue a very private life at her home by the sea.

One day a friend saw her sitting on the sea sands, her Bible in her lap, staring out into the glow of a beautiful sunset. The friend was invited to sit with her and as they talked, the friend asked, "How is it that you ever came to abandon the stage at the height of your success?"

Jenny Lind answered softly, "When every day it made me think less of this [laying a finger on her Bible] and nothing at all of that [pointing to the sunset], what else could I do?"

We must never expect another person to understand fully our personal faith and trust in God, or our desire to focus on spiritual things more than material things. We must never expect others to understand how we can trust God in the face of circumstances that cause them to feel dismay or fear.

A walk in faith is very personal—but never lonely, because God *always* walks with the faithful.

LIVE TRUE TO YOUR FAITH.

A New Start

"Do not remember the past events,
Pay no attention to things of old.
Look, I am about to do something new;
Even now it is coming."
(Isaiah 43:18–19)

By the time Paul Galvin was thirty-three years old, he had experienced two major financial failures. In the most recent failure, business competitors had forced him to fold his storage-battery business. Many people in his shoes would have quietly sought a job at a stable business owned and operated by others.

Galvin, however, believed in the product he had been manufacturing and selling, so he attended the auction of his own bankrupt business. With $750 he had managed to set aside, he bought back a portion of the inventory. And with that as his only material asset, he began to build a new company.

This "third time out," Galvin succeeded. He worked at the company he founded until retirement age. The firm became a household word: Motorola.

After he retired, Galvin said, "Do not fear mistakes. You will know failure—continue to reach out."

A preacher once voiced a similar word: "I may not see a soul saved every time I preach, but I will continue to preach. I may not see a person healed every time I pray for the sick at the local hospital, but I will continue to go there and pray. The next time I preach, the next time I pray, God just may choose to do the miraculous!"

The opposite of faith is fear. Fear cripples and often paralyzes faith. But fear cannot win completely as long as a person *chooses* to believe, and to act on that belief, trusting God to make a way in the face of any failure or disappointment. Indeed, a failure isn't really a failure until a person quits believing!

No matter what may have happened to you in the past, God has a success designed for your future. Believe for it, and *go* for it!

BUILD UP YOUR FAITH AND PUSH DOWN YOUR FEAR.

DAVID-STYLE FAITH

When the Philistine started forward
to attack him, David ran quickly to the
battle line to meet the Philistine.

(1 SAMUEL 17:48)

Sunday school teacher was teaching a series about King David. She began one lesson by focusing on the statement David made to King Saul about his having killed a young lion and a bear as he tended his father's sheep.

"For David to have been entrusted with the 'solo' care of the family flocks," the teacher said, "he most assuredly would have been a teenager, and what teenager shrinks from a challenge? What teenager thinks that a particular stunt is going to kill him, or a particular obstacle is capable of stopping him? I suggest to you that David might have said this to the lion and the bear that sought to steal and kill his sheep, 'You are going to die some way and some day—I'm here to make sure you die this way and today.'

"David *could* have run the other way when he saw the lion or the bear. He could have sacrificed a sheep to each of these predators and caused the rest of the flock to move quickly to safety. But David also knew that if he didn't kill the predators, they would strike again. That's what predators do—they stalk, and kill.

"And then the day came when David saw and heard Goliath, who in his mind was just another predator—this time a predator for the lives of people. While everyone else was saying, 'Goliath is too big to hit,' David probably said, 'He's too big to miss!'

"David ran *toward* predators, not away from them. And *that's* what faith does! Identify what is seeking to kill your potential, your enthusiasm, your marriage, your success—and run toward it with your faith in God. The Lord wants for *you* what a predator wants for himself."

RUN TOWARD WHAT THREATENS TO
DESTROY YOU——WITH FAITH.

WALKING THE WALK

Walk as children of light—for the fruit of the light results in all goodness, righteousness, and truth— discerning what is pleasing to the Lord.

(EPHESIANS 5:8–10)

Professional stock-car racer Darrell Waltrip once was very proud of his reputation as the "guy folks loved to hate." If a crowd booed, he'd just kick the dirt and smile.

Life changed for Waltrip when he miraculously survived a devastating Daytona 500 crash. He began attending church regularly with his wife, Stevie, and he and Stevie began to try to have a baby. They experienced four miscarriages, however. Waltrip, accustomed to "winning," felt as if he was now "losing."

The Waltrips' pastor came to visit one day. In their conversation, he called upon Waltrip to "walk the walk, not just talk the talk" in his faith. Waltrip had never thought about that. He began to question many areas of his life, including his ability to be a father. He asked himself, *What kind of dad would I be?*

He began to be more concerned about his reputation. He knew that children loved admiring his car, but the more he contemplated that, the more uncomfortable he became that his car was sponsored by a beer company. He asked himself, *Is this the image I want?*

Walking the walk involved choices and decisions he had never considered before!

Waltrip was thinking about how he might approach the owner of his car to find a new sponsor when an unexpected opportunity came his way to drive for a new racing team that was sponsored by a *laundry detergent* company! After much prayer, he switched teams. Two years later, daughter Jessica was born to the Waltrips, and a few years later, daughter Sarah. And then he won Daytona. Did these things happen after Waltrip began to walk the walk, not just believe and not just talk the talk of faith? He's convinced God was waiting to see what he would *do* with his faith.

FAITH IS MORE THAN A BELIEF OR A STATEMENT . . .
IT IS A SERIES OF CHOICES AND BEHAVIORS.

THE MOMENTS ADD UP

[Jesus said,] "His master said to him, 'Well done, good and faithful slave!'"

(MATTHEW 25:21)

Several centuries ago, the emperor of Japan commissioned a prominent Japanese artist to paint a particular species of bird for him. The emperor drew personal strength and inspiration from this bird and wanted a personal reminder of it in his palace.

An emperor's request is certainly not something to be ignored, but months—even years—went by without any word from the artist. The emperor finally decided to pay the man a personal visit to find out why he hadn't completed the painting.

The artist responded to the visit by putting a blank canvas on his easel. Within fifteen minutes, he had completed a painting of the bird. The emperor, admiring both the painting and the artist's great skill, declared it a masterpiece—and then asked the artist why he had delayed so long in putting brush to canvas.

Without saying anything, the artist went to several cabinets in his studio and began to pull arm loads of drawings and sketches of feathers, wings, claws, eyes, beaks—virtually every part of this particular species of bird, from virtually every angle. He placed these before the emperor, who examined each illustration and then nodded in silent understanding. Both artist and emperor knew that a magnificent "whole" of anything in life can never be greater than the magnificence of a single detail.

Focus on a moment, on the immediate opportunities and conversations. Seek to establish a singular expression of faith. Within your day, work to create an hour of focused belief, in which you speak faith-based words and do things that require an expression of faith. Seek to have a faith-filled *day* . . . and then a faith-filled *month* . . . and then a faith-filled *year.*

The key to a faith-filled life begins in the details of "right now."

INFUSE THE MOMENTS OF TODAY

WITH YOUR TRUST IN GOD.

A Vision for What Might Be

God has given us new life and light to our eyes.
(Ezra 9:8)

Several decades ago a man went with a friend for a ride out through the countryside a couple dozen miles from their respective homes. They drove off a main road and through a grove of orange trees. Horses grazed nearby, and a couple of ramshackle homes could be seen, but they appeared unoccupied.

Walter stopped the car and told his friend Arthur that he had purchased this particular plot of ground. Then he began to describe to his friend, in vivid detail, what he was going to build on the property. He encouraged his friend to buy the adjacent acreage. He said, "I can handle the main project myself. It will take all my money, but . . . I want you to have the first chance at this surrounding acreage, because in the next five years it will increase in value several hundred times."

Arthur considered his friend's proposition. He also asked himself, *Who in the world is going to drive twenty-five miles for his crazy project built out among the orange groves?* He truly thought his friend Walter, for all his brilliant artistic creativity, had lost his common sense on this particular venture. He finally said to Walter, "I'll consider this deal later." Walter replied, "You'd better move on it right now. Later will be too late."

Arthur failed to act. And Walter was right. Years later, Arthur—better known to the world as Art Linkletter—told audiences how he had turned down the opportunity to buy the land that surrounded what became Disneyland, the "project" his friend Walt Disney had envisioned for him.

Most opportunities in life require a person to act in faith and to see with eyes of hope and vision what does not yet exist.

LOOK AT OPPORTUNITIES WITH EYES OF FAITH TODAY.

POURING FAITH INTO A NEW GOAL

*[Jesus said,] "No one who puts his hand to the plow
and looks back is fit for the kingdom of God."*

(LUKE 9:62)

After ten years of being a physician, A. J. Cronin developed a very severe gastric ulcer. He was advised to leave his practice and the city for a time of "complete rest." He went to the Scottish Highlands to recuperate. He recalled later: "The first days of leisure were pleasant enough, but soon the enforced idleness of Fyne Farm became insufferable. . . . I had often, at the back of my mind, nursed the vague illusion that I might write. I had actually thought out the theme of a novel."

In his cold, clean, well-scrubbed room at the farm, Cronin had little furniture—but he did have a table with a very hard chair next to it. He had taken a small blank "exercise book" with him into recuperation, and one morning he found himself sitting in the hard chair, the exercise book open on the table, his pen in hand. He was keenly aware that he had never written anything of significance in his life other than what he called "dog-Latin prescriptions." Nevertheless, he began to write.

Cronin struggled to reach his personal goal of five hundred words a day—about a page and a half of printed text—and he later threw the first draft of his manuscript into the farm's trash pile. Eventually, however, he persevered and finished *Hatter's Castle.* The novel was translated into twenty-two languages, scripted for theatrical performance, and sold five million copies.

Are you applying your faith to the *project* that God has planted deep into the recesses of your own soul and spirit? Is God giving you an opportunity to explore, work on, and *do* something that is out of your comfort zone but definitely in a faith zone of obedience to the Lord?

TODAY IS A GOOD DAY TO START PURSUING
THE VISION YOU'VE BEEN IGNORING.

RENEWED EYES OF FAITH

Renew a steadfast spirit within me.

(PSALM 51:10)

A farmer once grew weary of the farm on which he had lived all his life. He knew it was a good farm, but he began to think, *Maybe there's more. I was born here and I've never known anything else. I should explore more of life's possibilities!* Soon after, he noted that every day, he seemed to find a new reason or two about why his old farm no longer excited him or fulfilled his expectations in life. He said, "I hadn't faced up to all the things that are wrong! I'm on the right track in wanting to trade this out for something better!" He finally decided to put place his farm for sale, and he sought out a well-known real estate broker in the area. He authorized him to place the farm on the market and to advertise it for sale.

The broker immediately prepared an advertisement listing the many advantages of the acreage:

Ideal location. Acres of fertile soil. Healthy livestock. Modern equipment. High yields on crops. Well-kept pens and barns. Attractive two-story house on a hill with a pleasant view of a pasture.

The broker went to the farmer to show him the advertisement before he placed it in the local newspaper. When the farmer finished reading it, he said, "Hold everything! I've changed my mind. I'm not going to sell. I've been dreaming of a place just like this!"

Rather than focus a critical eye on disappointments or difficulties, ask God to show you how *He* sees your life. Ask Him to reveal the potential you have not embraced, the opportunities that still exist. Ask Him to open your eyes of faith to your own marriage, family life, personal ministry, employment, neighborhood, and church. Begin to believe for God to work where you *are*.

ASK THE LORD TO RENEW YOUR EYES OF FAITH.

SEEING AS GOD SEES

*Let us run with endurance the race that lies before us, keeping
our eyes on Jesus, the source and perfecter of our faith.*

(HEBREWS 12:1-2)

John Ehrlichman was a convicted Watergate conspirator in the
1970s. He had a reputation as a brilliant lawyer and strategic
thinker . . . but that is not how he saw himself. He later wrote:

"When I went to jail, nearly two years after the cover-up trial, I had
a big self-esteem problem. I was a felon, shorn and scorned, clumping
around in a ragged old army uniform, doing pick and shovel work out
on the desert. I wondered if anyone thought I was worth anything.
For years I had been able to sweep most of my shortcomings and
failures under the rug and not face them, but during the two long
criminal trials, I spent my days listening to prosecutors tell juries
what a bad fellow I was. . . . I'd go back to a hotel room and sit alone
thinking about what was happening to me. During that time I began
to take stock. . . . I was wiped out. I had nothing left that had been of
value to me—honor, credibility, virtue, recognition, profession."

Then Ehrlichman began to see new things about himself. He
recognized that he cared deeply about his own integrity. He saw his
capacity to love and be loved. He wrote about his Nixon years and
his imprisonment years, "In a paradoxical way, I'm grateful for them.

Somehow I had to see all of that and grow to understand it in order to *arrive*."

From time to time, a person is wise to ask God, "How do *You* see me?" The Bible tells us that God desires for us to receive His love and to understand that He considers each of us to be an ongoing "creation under construction." He *believed in us*, long before we believed in Him.

HAVE FAITH IN GOD'S FAITH THAT YOU
ARE REDEEMABLE AND RENEWABLE!

Bottom-Line Faith

*[Jesus said,] "All the things you pray and ask for—believe
that you have received them; and you will have them."*

(MARK 11:24)

Ted enjoyed his visits to the home of his elderly great-uncle. Uncle Martin had been a missionary overseas for much of Ted's childhood, and Ted had always found his tales of missionary life both exciting and inspiring.

"You really faced just about everything out there on the mission field, didn't you?" he asked Uncle Martin on one visit. "I'm amazed you survived it all."

Uncle Martin chuckled. "Sometimes I'm amazed, too, Teddy."

They spent the next hour recalling a number of major life-threatening situations that Martin and his late wife, Louisa, had faced. They spoke of the time of severe drought that had resulted in severe food shortages and dried-up water sources. The drought and famine had produced death, and for those who had lived, economic hardship and, for many, serious illnesses. Literally hundreds of children and babies had died in the area of their small missionary clinic and church, and hundreds more women had experienced miscarriages. "And then there was the time when bands of political insurgents roamed the area, killing people at random," Martin recalled.

"And the time when a tiger entered the village," added Ted.

"And the time when your aunt Louisa became ill with a serious fever that never really was diagnosed."

"Not to mention the time a neighboring tribe went on a rampage and burned most of the homes in the village," Ted said.

"Or the time when a witch doctor came to our house and demanded that I heal his son or die."

"You had a lot of faith, Uncle Martin," Ted concluded. "You had faith to face so many things."

"Not really," replied his uncle. "I really only had faith for one thing."

"Just one?" Ted questioned. "What was that?"

"I had faith that God was in charge of all outcomes."

THE BOTTOM LINE FOR ALL FAITH IS THIS:
GOD IS SOVEREIGN OVER ALL THINGS.

A FAITH STORY

[Jesus said,]
"You will be My witnesses."
(ACTS 1:8)

"How was your weekend?" Pamela asked her business partner, Joanne, when she arrived at work on Monday morning.

"It was the most important weekend of my life," Joanne replied, adding, "at least so far."

"What happened?" Pamela asked eagerly. Joanne had been on a women's retreat with other women from her church.

"The speaker asked us to break into small groups on Saturday morning and to share what we considered to be our most profound faith story."

"What did you share?" Pamela asked.

"That's the point. I didn't have anything to share! The speaker had said that we were to share something in which we knew our faith had been involved—and tell what life was like before that time and then what life was like after. I couldn't think of a single experience in my life that qualified."

"Well, what about when you first invited the Lord to be your personal Savior—the time you accepted by faith that Jesus is the Son of God who died on the cross for your sins?" Pamela suggested.

Joanne grew very quiet. "I know you think I've done that, and you know I've gone to church regularly with my husband for years now, but the truth is, Pamela, that I had never done what you just said. I had never prayed and, with my faith, received Jesus as my Savior."

"Oh my," Pamela said softly.

"But I did this weekend!" Joanne exclaimed. "And *now* I have a faith story! I know what it means to feel absolutely clean in my spirit, and to be filled with a joy and a peace that I can't explain! I can hardly wait to use my faith in other ways the speaker suggested at the retreat! I want to become the queen of before-and-after faith stories!"

LOOK FOR AN OPPORTUNITY TO SHARE YOUR
FAITH STORY WITH SOMEONE TODAY.

A Prime Faith Moment

By faith we understand that the universe
was created by God's command, so that what is seen
has been made from things that are not visible.

(HEBREWS 11:3)

"Things still seem really bleak," Dorene confided to her older sister. Dorene's husband Mark had died six months before in a traffic accident.

"Are you doing the things you know to do to keep your faith alive?" her sister Verna asked. "Like going to church and reading the Bible and praying . . ."

"Yes," said Dorene. "But most of the time, I feel as if I'm just going through the motions. On some days, I have to read a verse in the Bible several times before I can fully concentrate on what I've read. And I'm not proud of the fact that yesterday, I reduced my prayers to just four words."

"What were they?" Verna asked.

"Do what You want," said Dorene with a grimace.

"Why, I think that's one of the best prayers you could ever have prayed!" Verna exclaimed.

"You do?" Dorene said. "I'm not sure I even meant it as a prayer. I had opened my Bible to read and decided I'd just start at the beginning. I only got through the first two verses." Dorene opened the Bible on the table next to her chair and read, 'In the beginning God created the heavens and he earth. Now the earth was formless and empty, darkness covered the surface of the watery depths, and the Spirit of God was hovering over the surface of the waters' (Genesis 1:1–2). She closed the book and said, "That's just the way I felt. Formless. Empty. Dark."

"I can hardly wait to see what God is going to speak into your life, Dorene," Verna said with great hope in her voice. "It will give you light. And it will be good! I just know it. You're on the brink of a creative act of God!"

GOD WANTS TO SPEAK INTO THE VOID
AND CHAOS OF YOUR LIFE TODAY.

Your Heroes of Faith

The world was not worthy of them.

(Hebrews 11:38)

*I*n many Bibles, the eleventh chapter of Hebrews is given the subtitle "Heroes of Faith." In this chapter, the writer of Hebrews tells how our spiritual ancestors in the Old Testament "won God's approval" by their faith.

Among those listed in the chapter are the following:

- Abel, who chose to offer God an acceptable sacrifice
- Enoch, whom God took directly to heaven
- Noah, who became an "heir of the righteousness that comes by faith"
- Abraham, who obeyed God's call to move by faith into a land of promise
- Sarah, who bore a child past normal child-bearing age
- Isaac, who passed on God's blessing and promises to Jacob and Esau
- Joseph, who prophesied the return of the Israelites to the land of promise
- Moses, who led his people out of Egypt
- And many others—Rahab, Gideon, Barak, Samson, Jephthah, David, Samuel, the prophets—all of whom lived faithful lives,

never living personally in the *fullness* of God's promises to His people but believing for them nonetheless

The heroes of faith applied their faith in different ways, for different purposes. Their reward, however, was the "approval" of God. In other words, God honored them and used their *believing* to empower their *doing*, and in the end, rewarded their lives with His eternal friendship.

Who are *your* heroes of faith? In what ways did their faith impact you?

Heroes are people we not only admire but desire to emulate. Are you becoming more and more like those you admire as your faith heroes?

Perhaps most importantly, do you know who is looking to *you* as a faith hero? Is your life one worth copying?

Being a "faith hero" is never easy. But it is perhaps the most important thing any person can aspire to be!

LIVE AS A FAITH HERO.

The Concert Surprise

*Humble yourselves, therefore,
under the mighty hand of God, so that
He may exalt you at the proper time.*

(1 Peter 5:6)

A mother once bought tickets to an Ignace Paderewski concert, hoping that the performance of this internationally famous pianist would inspire her young son to practice the piano more diligently. To be sure, the boy was enthralled at the sight of the nine-foot grand piano on the stage.

The mother began to talk to a friend in the row behind her, unaware that her son had slipped away and found the side steps to the stage. There, as the houselights began to dim and the spotlight fell on the piano, the boy climbed onto the piano bench and began to play "Twinkle, Twinkle, Little Star."

The mother was appalled, but as Paderewski took the stage, he moved quickly toward the boy and said, "Don't quit! Keep playing!" As the boy continued to play, Paderewski reached around him to his left to provide a base line of chords, and then he reached around him to his right to add a running obligato. Together, they thrilled the audience with a spontaneous and elaborate arrangement never performed before!

A reviewer later noted, "If Paderewski had not done what he did, there would have been no standing ovation. But if the boy had not done what he did, there would have been no musical magic at the opening of the concert."

You may think your faith is at the "beginner level." You may be reluctant to pray or act in faith. But be assured, as you seek to manifest the faith you have, Almighty God is wrapping His arms around you and addressing the need before you with *His* everlasting love.

You never act in faith alone. God's faith always joins your faith, and the combined effort is one that God ensures is *more than sufficient*.

PLAY THE NOTES YOU KNOW AND LEAVE
THE FINAL ARRANGEMENT TO GOD.

God's Divine Tugging

Today, if you hear His voice:
Do not harden your hearts.

(Psalm 95:7–8)

A young teenager accepted Jesus Christ as his personal Savior during a weekend revival meeting. The word spread quickly the next Monday morning, and several of his school friends questioned him during the noon recess.

"What did you do?" one of his friends asked.

"At the end of the sermon, I knew God wanted me to go forward to the altar and pray and ask Jesus to forgive me of my sins."

"How did you know God wanted you to do that? Did you hear God talk?" another friend asked.

"No," said the boy.

"Did you have a vision?" still another friend asked.

"No," said the boy.

"Then how did you *know* God wanted you to do that?"

The young teen thought for a moment and then said, "It's like when you go fishing. You can't see the fish in the water, or hear the fish, but you know when a fish takes the bait on your hook. You can feel him tugging on the end of your line. Well, I felt God tugging on my heart. He was reelin' me in!"

Too often, perhaps, we try to make "sense" of the way God works in our hearts. We try to "figure out" what God wants by analyzing a situation, making estimates, and calculating consequences. We must recognize that there is a level of truth that cannot be perceived by the five senses or measured objectively. It is at that level where faith operates in its fullness.

Faith compels us to *believe*, even against all logic at the time. It compels us to trust, even when we see no reason to trust.

Faith is the tug of God's infinite love on our lives, and in the end, it is what connects us to Him now and forever.

ASK GOD TO DRAW YOU CLOSER TO HIS HEART TODAY.

FAITH-INSPIRING
SCRIPTURES TO MEMORIZE

- God has distributed a measure of faith to each one (Romans 12:3).
- You are saved by grace through faith, and this is not from yourselves; it is God's gift—not from works, so that no one can boast (Ephesians 2:8–9).
- Without faith it is impossible to please God, for the one who draws near to Him must believe that He exists and rewards those who seek Him (Hebrews 11:6).
- Let us run with endurance the race that lies before us, keeping our eyes on Jesus, the source and perfecter of our faith (Hebrews 12:1–2).
- Faith is the reality of what is hoped for, the proof of what is not seen (Hebrews 11:1).
- By faith we understand that the universe was created by God's command, so that what is seen has been made from things that are not visible (Hebrews 11:3).
- [Jesus said,] If you believe, you will receive whatever you ask for in prayer (Matthew 21:22).
- Let him ask in faith without doubting. For the doubter is like the surging sea, driven and tossed by the wind. That person should not expect to receive anything from the Lord (James 1:6–8).

- If you confess with your mouth, "Jesus is Lord," and believe in your heart that God raised Him from the dead, you will be saved. One believes with the heart, resulting in righteousness, and one confesses with the mouth resulting in salvation. Now the Scripture says, Everyone who believed on Him will not be put to shame . . . for everyone who calls on the name of the Lord will be saved (Romans 10:9–11, 13).
- Trust in the LORD with all your heart, and do not rely on your own understanding; think about Him in all your ways, and He will guide you on the right paths (Proverbs 3:5–6).
- Faith comes from what is heard, and what is heard comes through the message about Christ (Romans 10:17).

NOTES

_____

_____

_____

_____

_____

_____

_____

_____

_____

_____

_____

If you enjoyed reading this book and/or
it made an impact on your life,
we would appreciate your feedback.
Please send your comments via e-mail to:
meadowsedgegroup@gmail.com
or write us at:

Meadow's Edge Group
P.O. Box 6947
Siloam Springs, AR 72761

LOOK FOR

DAYBOOK *of* HOPE

Available in 2015 at bookstores everywhere
and online at www.BHPublishingGroup.com